¦I	I'm asleep
¦^o	I'm snoring
:-/	I'm baffled
:c	I'm pouting
:-@	I'm screaming
:-!	I'm whispering
:-Q	I'm a smoker
:-?	I'm a pipe smoker
:-})	I'm wearing a moustache
=¦:-)	I'm wearing a top hat
*<:-)	I'm Santa Claus
+-(:-)	I'm the pope
5:-)	Elvis
7:^]	Ronald Reagan
&;^}	Bill Clinton
C¦:-=	Charlie Chaplin
d:-)	Baseball player
:-[	Vampire
:-E	Vampire in need of orthodontia
<:-I	Dunce
K:-)	Propeller head
:8)	Piggy
3:-o	Cow
:=8	Babboon
0-)	Cyclops
[]	Hugs…
:*	…and kisses

◆ ◆

For every kind of computer user, there is a SYBEX book.

All computer users learn in their own way. Some need straightforward and methodical explanations. Others are just too busy for this approach. But no matter what camp you fall into, SYBEX has a book that can help you get the most out of your computer and computer software while learning at your own pace.

Beginners generally want to start at the beginning. The **ABC's** series, with its step-by-step lessons in plain language, helps you build basic skills quickly. Or you might try our **Quick & Easy** series, the friendly, full-color guide.

The **Mastering** and **Understanding** series will tell you everything you need to know about a subject. They're perfect for intermediate and advanced computer users, yet they don't make the mistake of leaving beginners behind.

If you're a busy person and are already comfortable with computers, you can choose from two SYBEX series—**Up & Running** and **Running Start**. The **Up & Running** series gets you started in just 20 lessons. Or you can get two books in one, a step-by-step tutorial and an alphabetical reference, with our **Running Start** series.

Everyone who uses computer software can also use a computer software reference. SYBEX offers the gamut—from portable **Instant References** to comprehensive **Encyclopedias**, **Desktop References**, and **Bibles**.

SYBEX even offers special titles on subjects that don't neatly fit a category—like **Tips & Tricks**, the **Shareware Treasure Chests**, and a wide range of books for Macintosh computers and software.

SYBEX books are written by authors who are expert in their subjects. In fact, many make their living as professionals, consultants or teachers in the field of computer software. And their manuscripts are thoroughly reviewed by our technical and editorial staff for accuracy and ease-of-use.

So when you want answers about computers or any popular software package, just help yourself to SYBEX.

For a complete catalog of our publications, please write:
SYBEX Inc.
2021 Challenger Drive
Alameda, CA 94501
Tel: (510) 523-8233/(800) 227-2346 Telex: 336311
Fax: (510) 523-2373

SYBEX is committed to using natural resources wisely to preserve and improve our environment. As a leader in the computer book publishing industry, we are aware that over 40% of America's solid waste is paper. This is why we have been printing the text of books like this one on recycled paper since 1982.

This year our use of recycled paper will result in the saving of more than 15,300 trees. We will lower air pollution effluents by 54,000 pounds, save 6,300,000 gallons of water, and reduce landfill by 2,700 cubic yards.

In choosing a SYBEX book you are not only making a choice for the best in skills and information, you are also choosing to enhance the quality of life for all of us.

Your First Modem

Your First Modem

· ·

For Lana and her first modem (someday)

Sharon Crawford

Sharon Crawford

San Francisco • Paris • Düsseldorf • Soest

Acquisitions Editor: Rudolph S. Langer
Developmental Editor: Richard Mills
Editor: Brenda Kienan
Assistant Editors: Michelle Khazai, Valerie Potter, Kris Vanberg-Wolff
Technical Editor: Maryann Brown
Book Series Designer: Alissa Feinberg
Production Artist: Charlotte Carter
Technical Illustrator, Screen Graphics Artist: Cuong Le
Page Layout and Typesetter: Ann Dunn
Proofreaders/Production Assistants: Kristin Amlie, Sarah Lemas
Indexer: Ted Laux
Cover Designer: Design Site
Cover Photographer: David Bishop

Library of Congress Card Number: 93-87027
ISBN: 0-7821-1417-2

Manufactured in the United States of America
10 9 8 7 6 5 4 3 2 1

To Charlie, who makes all things possible

Acknowledgments

Every author includes a statement in the acknowledgments to the effect that making a book is a collaborative process and not a one-person show. This cliché has arisen because it is very, very true. Many people made contributions to this book. Among them are:

Brenda Kienan, who is that truly rare creature, a tender-hearted editor who made a positive effort not to make me feel like an idiot (even when I was being one).

Maryann Brown, the excellent technical editor.

Jon H. Jackson, Penny Giever, and Wayne Stewart of Intel Corporation; Pete Royston of Royston Development; Adam and Sara Viener, proprietors of the Cyberia BBS; Stephen Leitner of MicroWerks; Kathryn Woods at CompuServe; and Don Hinds of Zoom Telephonics, all of whom provided information and assistance.

Thanks go to the following people who provided me with phone numbers, technical information, and the benefit of their experiences all along the line: Richard Mills, Savitha Varadan, Michael Gross, Linda Gaus, Stefan Gruenwedel, Gene Sprung, Sandra Giles, Jeff Freeman, Tom Lichty, Ward Yelverton, Stephen Satchell, and the many wonderful people I "talked" to on CompuServe, America Online, DELPHI, and Prodigy.

Thanks also go to Rudolph S. Langer, Sybex Editor-in-Chief, who holds the world record for being thanked in the most computer books and deserves it; and to all the other wonderful people who helped produce this book: Alissa Feinberg, book designer; Cuong Le, technical illustrator, John Corrigan, screen graphics artist, Charlotte Carter, production artist; Michelle Khazai, Val Potter, and Kris Vanberg-Wolff, assistant editors; Ann Dunn, typesetter; Kristin Amlie and Sarah Lemas, proofreaders; and Ted Laux, indexer.

Table of Contents

Two
What You Need to Know

Three
Buying Your Modem

Part Two

Installing the Hardware and Software

Four

Installing an External Modem

Five

Installing an Internal Modem

Six

Getting Started with Software

Part Three

Getting Online

Seven

Prodigy

Eight

CompuServe

Nine

America Online

Ten

The Internet

Eleven

Bulletin Boards

Twelve

Sending and Receiving Files

Part Four

Taking Care of Business

Thirteen

E-Mail and Remote Computing

◆ ◆ ◆ ◆ ◆ ◆ ◆ ◆ ◆ ◆ ◆ ◆ ◆ ◆ ◆ ◆ ◆ ◆

Fourteen
Faxes and Voice Mail

Fifteen
Common Problems and Their Solutions

Part Five
Troubleshooting

◆ ◆ ◆ ◆ ◆ ◆ ◆ ◆ ◆ ◆ ◆ ◆ ◆ ◆ ◆ ◆ ◆ ◆ ◆ ◆

Sixteen
On-Line Tools and a Few Good Tips

Appendix A   229
The Hayes AT Command Set

Appendix B   237
Popular On-Line Services

Appendix C   241
Resource Guide

Glossary   247

Introduction

So here you are in the bookstore fingering various scary-looking tomes, trying to decide which book is for you. Maybe you've bought a new computer with a modem already installed and you're wondering how to use it. Or someone pretending to be your friend sold you his old modem when he bought a new one and you're wondering if it has a use beyond that of paperweight.

Maybe you've been seeing ads on television or stories in magazines touting some amazing communications services and you'd like to take a look.

If this sounds like you, look no further. This book is definitely the one you want, because it will show you all the great ways you can expand your horizons via the telephone—in normal language.

Only a few years ago, modems were temperamental, quirky devices. You had to have a strong streak of masochism to even attempt to get one to work. That's not true any more. Today, lots of thoroughly normal people use modems to do all sorts of things. You can buy a shirt, make airline reservations, send mail, and discuss your cat's neuroses with people who won't think *you're* nuts, too. You can find out the weather in Poughkeepsie, stock prices in Tokyo, and the balance in your own bank account.

You can get lots of interesting software, play games with people you've never met, and find answers to questions you scarcely knew existed.

Aside from all the fun stuff, you can also send and receive faxes, send proposals to customers virtually anywhere, and conduct any business that does not actually *require* face-to-face contact.

Anything you can do with your computer also can be done across telephone lines with *another* computer.

 **NOTE**

MODEM stands for MOdulator-DEModulator. It converts the digital signals of your computer into analog signals that the phone company can handle across their wires and switches.

Who's This Book For?

Admittedly, using a modem is sort of a psychological Great Leap Forward for most people. However, no great technical expertise is needed. Like most computer-related subjects, you can get down-and-dirty if you really want to, but it is certainly possible to happily use a modem for years without having to dabble in the arcane arts.

This book assumes you're a reasonably intelligent person but not a computer whiz. I'll also assume that you have a computer you've used at least a little while, and that you either have a modem or are poised (credit card in hand) to acquire one. I'm also assuming that you're interested in *what* a computer and modem can do for you, not necessarily *how* it does it, so I won't go into any more technical detail than is absolutely necessary.

What's in This Book?

The book is divided into five parts. You certainly don't have to read them in order. Just take a look at the part or parts that apply to your interests. I place a big emphasis in this book on how to use every service as cheaply as possible. The one downside of on-line services is their potentially *very* high cost, so tips on how to keep that cost down are generously sprinkled throughout the text.

Part One: Before You Buy

The first part of the book covers the basic decisions you need to make before you buy a modem or fax/modem. Chapter 1 translates all the jargon you see in modem ads and tells you which stuff matters and which stuff is unimportant. Also in this chapter is information on how to choose among different types of modems and what the advantages and disadvantages of the various types are.

Chapter 2 reviews some of the things you need to think about before buying a modem. It covers computer hardware questions as well as how to use a modem on your phone line without driving yourself (and others) crazy.

In Chapter 3, there's some good advice on the pluses and minuses of buying your modem by mail versus at a local store. Here you'll find descriptions of what you can expect to get when you buy a modem, what you'll have to pay extra for, plus dollars-and-sense information on the costs of operating your modem.

Part Two: Installing the Hardware and Software

Here's where we get down to business. The chapters here have specifics on how to install an external modem and how to install an internal one. There's information on how to get the modem up and running with the software that comes with it and a discussion of various communications packages—their strengths and weaknesses, too.

Part Three: Getting Online

This is the biggest part of the book because, after all, this is probably why you want a modem in the first place. There are whole chapters here on CompuServe, Prodigy, America Online, the information highway known as the Internet, and more.

The emphasis here is on *specific* information on each service, exactly how you get to each one, and the ways to use each one effectively. Every chapter includes lots of money-saving tips and shortcuts.

This section also has a chapter on how to find and use bulletin boards, of which there are thousands. There's also a chapter on transferring files so you can exchange files and programs directly with another computer.

Part Four: Taking Care of Business

You'll find stuff in this section of particular interest to people using a modem for business operations.

Chapter 13 discusses the various e-mail services available. You'll also find information on remote computing. This is when you use your modem at home, for example, to sign on to another computer (let's say, your computer at work).

Even if you use your fax modem just to order pizza or send in your opinions to talk-radio shows, you'll still find useful information in the chapter on faxes. This section will also give you information on computer-based voice mail systems.

Part Five: Troubleshooting

With any luck at all, you'll never need to use this section. But if your luck runs out, see Chapter 15 for answers to some of the most common (and some not-so-common) questions and problems that can happen when communicating online.

Also in this section is Chapter 16, a summary of the on-line tools and tips that everyone eventually learns about—usually through trial-and-error and general stumbling about. Read this chapter and you'll have a head start on becoming a savvy user.

Other Stuff

I've included a detailed glossary at the end, defining all those pesky communication terms in normal English. There's also an appendix covering common commands of the Hayes command set (don't worry about what that is until you've read the book), an appendix of phone numbers for the most popular on-line services, and an appendix listing the addresses and phone numbers of the companies that supply the hardware and software mentioned in the text.

Getting the Show on the Road

In this book, you should be able to find everything you need to get started in the world of telecomputing. This won't make you an expert, but it'll point you in the direction of where-the-experts-are should you need to avail yourself of their services.

The idea is to give you a simple, direct start. Once you're launched, you'll be in the best position to decide where you want to go next. This book is meant to be the launching pad.

Let's Talk

If there's anything you'd like to suggest in the way of additions or corrections to this book, you can send them to me online (or at least, you'll be able to after reading the book). My online address is:

CompuServe: 76216,1463

I come and go on other services; CompuServe is the place I visit most often. If you're not on CompuServe, you can send mail to me from other services, by using the Internet address:

76216.1463@compuserve.com

If you have questions that aren't answered in this book, I most likely won't know either, but I can probably give you an idea where to look for answers. In any case, I *love* to get e-mail, so don't hesitate!

Hope you enjoy the book. I know you'll enjoy exploring the great big electronic world of computer communications waiting out there. The sooner you get started, the more fun you'll have. See you online!

Part One

Before You Buy

• •

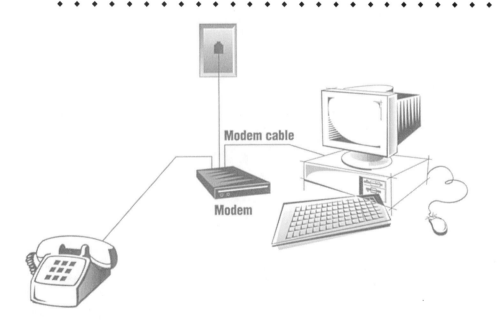

Modem cable

Modem

One

True Facts about Modems

• •

A *modem* is simply a piece of computer hardware that translates information produced by your computer into impulses that can be sent along regular telephone lines. At the other end of the line, another modem receives the impulses and translates them back into a language that the receiving computer can understand. Out of that simple process has grown the enormous world of computer telecommunications.

To join that world, you'll need not only a modem but also some software to do the actual translating. The software can range from extremely rudimentary (the software that comes with the modem) to extremely sophisticated (software you have to acquire separately). The software side of the equation is covered in more detail in Chapter 6.

This chapter covers the basics of modems—in particular, what all that jargon in the ads and on the boxes really means, which stuff is important, and which stuff is just there to impress the tourists.

Speed: What Do Those Numbers Mean?

Speed is the drug of choice among computer enthusiasts. The more you have, the more you want. As a result, the general rule is to get the fastest gadget you can afford—whether it's a modem, a printer, or a processor—because the sad fact is that however astonishingly fast it seems now, it'll probably feel very slow in a year or two.

 NOTE

You'll sometimes see the speed of modems described in "baud." While this isn't the same as **bits per second** (bps), in real life the terms can be considered interchangeable. However, to be excruciatingly correct, you should use **bps** when describing the speed of modems these days.

A modem's speed describes how many bits per second (bps) it can transmit. It's not complicated. The bigger the number, the faster the data moves, and the less time you will have to pay for if you are using a timed on-line service. A 9600bps modem can transmit four times as fast as a 2400bps modem, for example.

Today, the fastest modems used for ordinary transactions are 14,400bps (also shown as 14.4Kbps), and that's what you should buy. A 14.4Kbps modem will cost only $25 to $75 more than a 9600bps modem and is 50 percent faster.

Most on-line services top out today at 9600bps, though that's also changing very quickly. Many private bulletin boards (BBSs) support 14,400bps. All modems can easily "talk down" to lower speeds, but when you want to transmit data from a service where they're charging you by the minute or over a long-distance line, you'll want to move that data as fast as you can. That's where a high-speed modem earns back its slightly higher purchase price very quickly.

BPS versus Throughput

Just to confuse the issue a bit more, there's the question of *bits-per-second* versus something called *throughput*. Bits-per-second is just what it sounds like: the number of bits transmitted by a modem each second. Throughput, however, is a measure of the number of *useful* data bits transmitted each second. These two numbers are not necessarily identical.

With the use of file compression, modems can encode data, removing or condensing characters. The receiving modem then reconstitutes the data back to its original size. This means, for example, that 1,024 characters can be transmitted to represent a 2,048 character file. Therefore, if 1,024 characters are sent in a second, the effective useful data transfer rate was 2,048bps.

Theoretically, a modem using the V.42bis standard can achieve a throughput up to four times its transmission speed. This means a 14,400bps modem can have a throughput up to 57,600bps, even though it can still transmit no more than 14,400 bits per second.

Modems with fax capability are sometimes shown with two numbers: one for the speed at which faxes are transmitted and one for the speed at which everything else happens. If you're likely to be sending and receiving faxes on a regular basis, get a fax modem that transmits *both faxes and data* at the highest possible speed.

On the other hand, if your on-line activity is limited to the sending and receiving of infrequent e-mail, an older, slower modem will do the job. You can pick up a used 2400bps modem from a friend or in the classifieds for less than $50. The fact is, however, that almost any user will benefit from having a faster modem.

 TIP

Today, most of the 14,400bps modems are made with chips manufactured by Rockwell International. A modem with the Rockwell chip set will have built-in fax capability, so you won't save any money by getting a 14,400bps **without** fax capability.

Modem Talk Translated Here

Modems are surrounded by just as much jargon and mystifying mumbo-jumbo as any other aspect of computers. Much of that, however, was only relevant in the bad old days of telecommunications and can be safely ignored today.

Hayes Compatibility

Some years ago, a company called Hayes Microcomputer Products produced a series of modems that responded to a specific set of computer-generated commands. These commands have become the standard for all modems produced for the general marketplace today. In fact, they're so standard that most advertisements no longer even mention whether a modem is Hayes-compatible.

 **NOTE**
The curious will find information about the Hayes AT command set in Appendix A.

If you buy your modem from any major manufacturer, it will definitely be Hayes-compatible, whether the ad says so or not. If you have any doubts, *ask,* because a modem that *isn't* Hayes-compatible has no use beyond that of paperweight.

Asynchronous? Synchronous?

Sometimes an advertisement or magazine story will make a point of saying that a given modem will communicate in both *asynchronous* and *synchronous* modes. This isn't really important because virtually all modem communications are done *asynchronously*.

If you need synchronous transmission (which is used for communicating with mainframe computers and over leased lines), you'll know. You'll also pay quite a bit extra for a modem that can transmit synchronously. So, unless you need to connect with your company's IBM System/390 or AS/400, an asynchronous modem will do just fine.

Full-Duplex and Half-Duplex

A modem that operates at *full-duplex* can send and receive data simultaneously. A modem that operates at *half-duplex* can send or receive information, but cannot do both at the same time.

It's very difficult to even find a half-duplex modem these days. You certainly wouldn't want to buy one (or even take one for free). The only reason this still comes up is that most communications software allows you to set up for half-duplex operation—but it's extremely unlikely that you'd ever need to do so.

What's This V. Business?

One tricky fact about modems is that it always takes two to tango. That is, your modem can't dance without a partner modem at the other end of the phone line—and not just any modem, either. It has to be one that speaks the same language as yours. As a result, the issue of transmission standards is very important.

Somewhere out there is an outfit called CCITT (*Comité Consultatif International Télégraphie et Téléphonie*), and it's a good thing, too! This body is responsible for setting a whole series of international standards for data communications. Each series is designated by a letter; many of those in the V series deal with modems. This is why you see things like "V.32" and "V.42bis" in the modem advertisements. These notations refer to the standards set by the CCITT regarding speed, error-checking, and data compression.

Most of these numbers (every modem box has loads of them) mean nothing to the vast majority of users, but there are some you'll need to know about. For a listing of the essential numbers for a 9600bps modem, see Table 1.1. For a 14,400bps modem, see Table 1.2.

 NOTE

Some people will try to tell you "bis" is French for **second!** But I know you're too smart to believe that. The "bis" in V.32bis (and so forth) is from the Latin and means **the second iteration** of that standard. So V.32bis is the second version of V.32.

Table 1.1

What should be on the box (or in the ad) when you are buying a 9600bps modem

Essential Standard	What It Means
V.32	Will operate at 9600bps
V.42bis	Can reach throughput up to 38,800bps
MNP-5	Includes error-checking and data-compression protocols
Hayes-compatible	Will work with most software

Table 1.2

What should be on the box (or in the ad) when you are buying a 14,400bps modem

Essential Standard	What It Means
V.32bis	Will operate at 14,400bps, as well as at slower rates
V.42bis	Can reach throughput of 57,600bps
MNP-5	Includes error-checking and data-compression protocols
Hayes-compatible	Will work with most software

 NOTE

If you want to be able to use your modem to communicate with someone who uses a TDD terminal (those special terminals the phone company provides to the deaf and others who can't use standard phones), you'll want a modem that supports the Bell 103 standard.

The other numbers are there mostly to dress things up. For example, an advertisement for a 14,400bps modem may say that it adheres to the following standards: V.42bis, V.42, V.32bis, V.32, V.22bis, V.22, V.21, Bell 212A, and Bell 103.

Wow, is that impressive or what?

The fact is that the V.42 standard is included as part of V.42bis, V.22 is included as part of V.22bis (and just means the thing will operate at both 2400bps and 1200bps). V.21 means it will also work at 300bps, and the two Bell standards will allow you to communicate with some hard-copy terminals that are (to put it mildly) uncommon.

In other words, most of this stuff is redundant and just there to dazzle the rubes. All the numbers you really want to be sure of seeing are in Tables 1.1 and 1.2. If the modem you're buying includes those standards, it'll include all the ones you need as well.

For a deciphering of most of the codes you're likely to see on a modem's packaging or in an advertisement, see Table 1.3.

Table 1.3

Deciphering the standards

Standard	Covers	BPS	Comments
V.21	Speed	300	A very early standard
V.22, Bell 212A	Speed	1200	Most common standard for 1200bps modems
V.22bis	Speed	2400	First true world standard, introduced in 1984
V.32	Speed	4800,9600	Now being replaced by V.32bis
V.32bis	Speed	14,400	Includes the rates supported by V.32
V.32*terbo*	Speed	19,200	Not an approved standard, but a lot of modems are out there with this designation
V.42	Error correction		Designed to make communications more reliable
V.42bis	Data compression		Can increase throughput by as much as four times the nominal modem speed
V.FastClass	Speed	28,800	Not approved—companies selling it *say* it will work with V.Fast—be suspicious!
V.Fast (will be V.34)	Speed	28,800	The current name for the new standard expected to be approved in mid-1994
V.17	Fax speed	14,400	Permits fax transmission and reception at 14.4Kbps

How Fast is V.fast?

A new standard of 28,800bps is expected to be approved around mid-1994. When approved, it will be under the name V.34. In the meantime, modems that conform to the expected standard are being sold under the name V.Fast. As of now, exceeding the speeds provided by a 14,400bps modem requires proprietary transmission protocols. In other words, you have to have the same kind of modem at both ends of the transmission. This will still be true for a while even after V.34 is approved and there are enough 28,800bps modems in circulation for the standard to be widely accepted.

The faster-than-14,400bps modems now available command a premium price—$500 and up.

MNP

MNP (short for Microcom Networking Protocol), represents a set of error-correcting and data-compression techniques. These protocols are programmed into a modem's chips, so the box should tell you which ones are present.

MNP-1 is not particularly important. MNP-2 through MNP-4 are present in virtually all new high-speed modems. (Note that if your modem supports the V.42 standard, MNP2-4 are there whether the box says so or not.)

Look for a modem with MNP-5. This protocol includes data-compression techniques that can dramatically increase the speed at which data is transmitted. The presence of MNP-5 also indicates that the lower-numbered MNPs are there, too.

External and Internal Modems

Modems can be bought as *external* devices that plug into the back of your computer or as *internal* boards that go inside your computer box. Both kinds work essentially in the same way, but there are enough fringe differences to incline you to prefer one or the other.

External Modems

External modems come in their own little plastic box—usually no bigger than this book. They'll have a series of lights in the front and connections in the back. The modem shown in Figure 1.1 is a 14.4Kbps external modem from Practical Peripherals.

Figure 1.1

A sleek 14.4Kbps fax modem. The slots in the top are for the speaker, so you can hear the connection being made (if you want to).

External modems are certainly the simplest to install. You just plug them in. An external modem will need to be connected to:

- A serial port in the back of your computer
- The phone line
- A power outlet

Other positive attributes of the external modem are that it's easily portable (you can unplug it from one computer and plug it into another), and it has indicator lights that can tell you what's going on. (Is data being received or sent? Is the line open?)

On the debit side of the ledger, an external modem:

- Requires its own source of electricity (so you have to find a place to plug it in)
- Requires its own serial port (so if you only have one and it's being monopolized by your mouse, you'll need to either add a serial port or buy an internal modem)
- Takes up desk space
- Is more susceptible to damage by passing children/animals/ cans of soda
- Costs slightly more than an internal modem

How Great UART

The circuit that controls the serial port on your computer is on a chip called "UART" (Universal asynchronous receiver/transmitter). You need a fast UART if you're going to be using a fast modem (9600bps or faster).

External modems use the UART attached to the serial port on your computer. If you have an older computer, the older UART may impair the performance of your new, high-speed modem (particularly if you'll be using Windows communications software). The older UARTs have either the number 8250 or 16450. The newer UARTs are identified by either the number 16550 or 16550A.

If you have the older UART and are determined to have a high-speed external modem, you can replace the serial port on your computer. Or you can take the easy way out and buy an internal modem that comes with its own UART and, in effect, provides its own serial port.

To find out which UART you have, you can run the Microsoft Diagnostics program, MSD (found in your Windows, DOS6, or Windows for Workgroups directory), or, if you have Norton Utilities 7, run the program NDIAGS and select Hardware Configuration from the File menu.

Internal Modems

An internal modem comes as a circuit board that fits into one of your computer's expansion slots. (An example of an internal fax modem is shown in Figure 1.2.) As you can probably imagine, that's the internal modem's greatest weakness: you have to open up the computer box to install it. If the thought of doing that doesn't nauseate you (or if, even better, you can get someone else to do it), buy an internal modem.

Reasons for preferring an internal modem are:

- It's tucked away inside the box, so it doesn't require an external electrical supply or cable
- It's safe from spills and dust
- It will have its own UART chip to prevent data loss (see the boxed text titled "How Great UART" earlier in this chapter)

On the other hand, it won't have those reassuring lights to gaze at, and it's not exactly portable.

Again, your choice (to use an external or internal modem) should be based on which of the factors described above means the most to you. There's no difference in real performance between internal and external modems.

 NOTE

If you travel a lot with your laptop, you're much better off with an internal modem designed specifically for that computer. That will cut down on the number of cords and cables and other junk you have to remember to pack.

Figure 1.2
This is an internal modem (one that goes inside your computer box). It has a speaker, like the external modems, but no signaling lights.

What about Fax Modems?

Fax capability on a modem used to be an exotic luxury (only a couple of years ago). It cost a lot more and didn't work all that well. Now virtually all high-speed modems are available with fax capability built in. They cost no more with fax included and work very well indeed.

In fact, you really have to look long and hard now for a high-speed modem *without* fax capability. You may have to buy extra software to actually send and receive faxes, but if you look around you'll often find that the manufacturers will throw it in for under $50 (or even for free).

Just be sure that the fax capability on your modem supports Group 3 fax transmission standards at the same speed as the modem. In other words, if the modem's top speed is 9600bps, the fax part should also transmit *and* receive at 9600bps.

Fax Modem or Fax Machine?

Since the modem you buy will undoubtedly be able to send and receive faxes, does this mean it's a satisfactory substitute for a freestanding fax machine?

Maybe.

If you receive a lot of faxes and you don't want to spring for a plain-paper fax machine ($700 and up—*way* up), a fax modem can be a good solution. However, you'll have to leave your computer on during all the hours that faxes may come in. If the faxes are arriving on your one and only computer while you're trying to use it, you'll also have to spring for a more expensive modem with its own coprocessor chip, so the faxes can arrive "in the background" and not interrupt your work. (You'll find more on these fancy devices in Part Four, "Taking Care of Business.")

But buying a modem with that coprocessor chip will still be cheaper than buying a freestanding machine and you won't have to deal with the nasty thermal paper used by most fax machines. With a fax modem you can print out your incoming faxes on your own printer using normal printer paper.

If you send a lot of faxes, a fax modem can also be a great choice. You can generate documents on your computer and send them off in a flash. With the right software (such as WinFax) you can even do "mass mailings" directly to other fax machines. Since the quality of a fax is determined by the sending machine, your faxes will be as good as they can be.

On the other hand, if you need to fax documents or pictures that were not generated on your computer, you'll still need either a freestanding fax machine or a *scanner* (a device that can "scan" materials and turn their images into "pictures" inside your computer).

In any case, the cost of fax capability in a modem is negligible, so you might as well do it. Depending on your needs, it may be enough (or more than enough) or you may want a freestanding machine as well.

A Final Note

Now that you've read this chapter, you're in a better position to determine what kind of modem you want and how to extract the information you need from all the jargon in the advertisements.

It's important to read ads for modems carefully, because so many numbers and weird terms are involved. You can easily overlook the critical information, which is: how fast does this modem send and receive data (and faxes), and will it work with all the other modems in the world?

In the next chapter, we'll talk about other factors you need to take into consideration before you actually buy and install your modem.

Two

What You Need to Know

. . . .

A certain amount of planning before you get your modem will help to make it work with your computer and phone system. The first part of this chapter covers what you need to know about your computer hardware. A later section on phone lines will help you and your modem peacefully coexist with other members of your household.

About Your Computer

A simple modem designed only to send messages hither and yon doesn't require a fancy computer setup. In fact, you can run almost any modem attached to almost any computer. But adding *any* piece of hardware to your system (not to mention the software to operate it) has implications that have to be considered.

Making Room on the Hard Drive

No matter how you plan to use your modem, you'll need to make some room on your hard drive. The telecommunications software alone may take 2- or 3MB. Some software, like Intel's Faxability Plus, takes up to 5MB of space. Understand, that's just the *software* to run your modem or fax/modem; it doesn't include any files or faxes created or received.

Faxes you receive (and keep) also take up room. A fax is actually a picture of the page, or pages, of the document that's sent to you. Most fax software saves the image in a format that may be 50K in size or 200K or even larger. If you accumulate many faxes, you'll find your hard drive getting crowded.

If you just intend to receive a fax or message, look at it once and then delete it, you can get away with less space.

Some fax software comes with Optical Character Recognition (OCR) software, which can be used to convert the image of a printed page back into text. This can save as much as 75 percent of the storage space, but the accuracy of the conversion may be fairly lousy, depending on the quality of the received fax.

Some software may also let you convert faxed graphics to a format (such as TIFF, EPS, BMP, or such) that you can then manipulate. These converted files also require hard drive space, depending on how complex the image is.

So, if you're going to be saving a few faxes and a modest number of files, you won't need more than about 2MB of free hard-disk space beyond that required by the modem software.

If you don't have enough free space on your hard disk, you can do one of the following:

- Delete old files or back them up onto floppies
- Buy and use a disk-compression program (such as Stacker) or use the disk-compression utility that comes with DOS 6
- Buy a bigger hard disk

If none of those will do, you can faithfully save the faxes and files you want to keep by backing them up onto floppies when you've finished with them and then delete them from your hard drive.

What about Memory?

Memory is an issue you'll have to address only for the software you'll be using. Be sure to check the software's box for the system requirements.

Generally it's not a problem, but sometimes you will need to know how much memory and what type you have in your computer. For example, if you're using WordPerfect 6.0 for DOS with fax capability, you'll need enough memory (that can be configured as Expanded memory) to use the fax function from within WP.

To find out how much memory you have, you can use the MS-DOS program named MSD.EXE (Microsoft Diagnostics). Just type **MSD** at the DOS prompt. Or watch the startup screen when you boot your computer. Another way to check your memory is to type **MEM** at the DOS prompt, and you'll see a screen like the one shown in Figure 2.1.

What's a Port and Why Do I Have to Be Bothered?

Another important question is how many *serial ports* you have in your computer. A *port* is a connecting point on your computer for hooking up external devices and generally refers to either *parallel* or *serial* ports. Parallel ports typically use 25 *pins* (wires) to pass a batch of signals

Figure 2.1

The MEM program will tell you all about the memory in your computer.

```
C:\>mem

Memory Type         Total =   Used +   Free
---------------     ------    ------   ------
Conventional         640K      150K     490K
Upper                  0K        0K       0K
Adapter RAM/ROM      128K      128K       0K
Extended (XMS)      7424K     2912K    4512K
---------------     ------    ------   ------
Total memory        8192K     3190K    5002K

Total under 1 MB     640K      150K     490K

Total Expanded (EMS)                    7744K (7929856 bytes)
Free Expanded (EMS)                     4512K (4620288 bytes)

Largest executable program size          490K (501280 bytes)
Largest free upper memory block            0K     (0 bytes)
MS-DOS is resident in the high memory area.

C:\>
```

concurrently across the cables between the computer and the device at the other end. Parallel ports are used primarily with printers.

Serial ports are the connection points for modems, a mouse or other pointer device, a few weird types of printers, and some other hardware. A serial connector may have either nine or 25 pins, though not all of the pins are necessarily used.

Most PCs today come with two serial ports. (You can get more, but that's not standard issue.) If you have only one serial port, it's possible that your mouse may already be plugged into it.

Even if you have only one connector for a serial port on the back of the computer, another port may be made accessible simply by adding another connector from inside of the computer to the outside, or by adding a couple of chips and a connector. It's also both simple and cheap to have another serial port installed. You can even buy one at the same time you buy your modem, then bribe a knowledgeable friend to install them both! (If you watch closely, you'll see how easy it is and do it yourself ever after.)

You can determine how many serial ports are on your computer either by looking or by using software. As mentioned earlier, many systems tell you what's installed in the computer when the computer starts up; you can simply check at startup to see how many serial ports are mentioned, or you can use the diagnostic program MSD to see what ports and other devices are seen by the system. The MSD report is shown in Figure 2.2.

NOTE

Parallel ports are also referred to as **LPT** ports. Serial ports are also called **COM** ports.

NOTE

If you have, or intend to get, an internal modem, it is not necessary to have two external serial ports on your computer. Internal modems have their own serial chip set on the modem card.

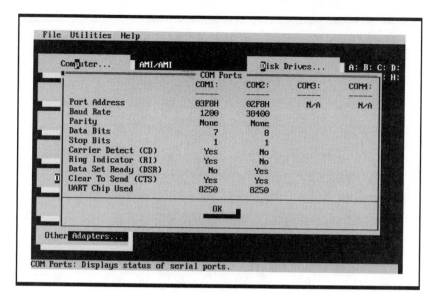

Figure 2.2
The Microsoft Diagnostics COM
Port screen

You can also look at the back of your computer to see how many serial connectors are on the back. Take a good look at all the stuff on the back of your computer. Disregard where the monitor and printer are plugged in.

You'll see some plugs (in other words, ports). Some will be small and have nine connector pins. These are called nine-pin connectors (or DB9). There may also be one or more 25-pin connectors (DB25).

The nine-pin connectors are serial ports. The 25-pin connectors can be either serial or parallel ports.

You can tell whether a 25-pin port is series or parallel by examining whether it's male or female. (Relax, this is not as much fun as it sounds. The terminology is merely sexist, not sexy.) Parallel ports on a machine have what are known as *female* connectors, that is, sockets that the pins of a cable are stuck into.

Serial ports have *male* connectors—a series of pins sticking out. The cables you plug into a serial port are always female. Figure 2.3 shows the two kinds of cable connectors (nine- and 25-pin) that connect to serial ports.

 NOTE

Serial ports are commonly used for connecting the mouse, but some systems come with what's called a **mouse port** specifically for the mouse. This kind of port uses a round eight-pin connector that doesn't look anything like either a serial or a parallel port. An advantage to having a mouse port is that you don't use up a serial port that you may want for a modem or another toy.

Figure 2.3
The serial ports on your
computer will correspond to
one of these types of cable
connectors.

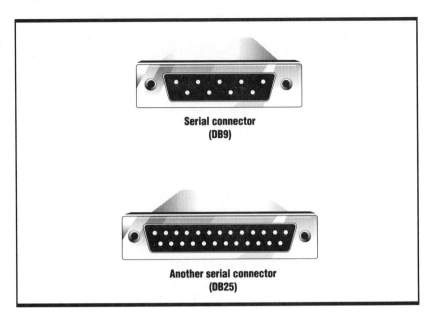

Serial connector
(DB9)

Another serial connector
(DB25)

Getting More Ports

Even if you have two installed serial ports already being used by other
devices, it's still possible to use a modem with your computer.

One method for accomplishing this is to use a switch box with an
external modem, so you can switch between devices sharing a port. A
simple A-B switch box is cheap and easy to install, though it is a pain
to always have to remember to turn on the device you want to be the
active one.

Another approach is to take advantage of the fact that your PC's setup
may allow you to have up to four serial ports. Serial ports are designated as COM1, COM2, COM3, and COM4. You can configure one of
the extra devices to be on COM3 or COM4.

Naturally, it's not quite as simple as that. Each COM port has associated
with it something called a hardware interrupt (abbreviated "IRQ").
This is an electronic signal that the device on the port sends to the
main part of the computer to get its attention (sort of like pulling the
emergency cord on a train). No two devices can use the same IRQ at
the same time. COM1 and COM3 both are assigned IRQ4. COM2 and
COM4 are assigned IRQ3.

This makes things a bit trickier. If you just assign your modem to COM3 while your mouse is on COM1, your mouse will definitely not work while you're using your modem. They'll probably both flake out.

Fortunately, most devices allow you to set interrupts while you're setting the COM port. One common solution is to assign IRQ5 (which is normally used by LPT2, the second printer port) to COM3. Unless you have a printer on that port, you can use IRQ5 without a problem.

Some modems, such as the SatisFAXtion fax modems made by Intel, will figure out their own solutions. The setup software automatically detects what you have installed in your computer and suggests a setting for you to use.

WARNING

IRQ5 is often used by network cards as well. If you're on a network, get the advice and help of the network administrator before trying to co-opt any interrupt for use with your modem.

All about Phone Lines

You don't have to install a separate telephone line for your modem; sharing is not only possible but easy. You will have to make sure that your outlet has standard RJ-11 plugs—the kind common to most telephone systems in North America—because your modem will be set up to plug in using RJ-11 connectors both at the wall and at the modem.

If your phone system doesn't have RJ-11 connectors, take this opportunity to convert the existing connectors. All telephone and Radio Shack stores sell conversion kits that are inexpensive and easy to use.

Sharing the Line with Other People

One hazard of sharing a phone line is that someone will pick up an extension phone while you're using your modem and cause your connection to go kablooey. You can deal with this in one of two ways:

- Warn others in your household when you're going to be using your modem and make appropriate threats
- Buy a device that keeps extension phones from butting in when you're online

I use the second approach, with a device called The Stick (manufactured by Multi-Link, Inc.). The modem plugs into The Stick and it, in turn, plugs into the telephone outlet. Someone picking up an extension hears that the line is being used but doesn't interfere with the transmission. It's a bit of work to set up (though not overly difficult), but it works very well.

Once you buy a modem and register it, you'll get lots and lots of catalogs in the mail. Among them will be catalogs full of other devices that enable you to share a phone line with a minimum of discomfort.

Sharing the Line with a Phone

The simplest way to share the line between a modem and a telephone is to plug both into one of those little single-line splitters like the one shown in Figure 2.4. Just plug the splitter into the wall outlet, then the modem into one socket and the phone into the other.

In most cases, you're better off plugging the phone into the appropriate socket in the back of the modem. This is particularly true if you have a fax modem. With this setup, the modem determines whether an incoming call is a fax, or a voice- or modem-call, and does the appropriate switching.

When you use automatic dialing programs, the software will tell you when to pick up the phone.

Figure 2.4
A simple solution for less than a buck

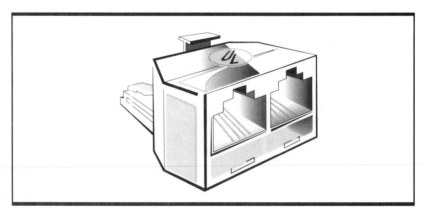

Sharing the Line with a Fax Machine

The only complication that can arise when a modem and a fax machine share a line is when both are in auto-answer mode. Both will try to answer any incoming call and things may get messy. This, however, is a highly unusual state of affairs. Under most circumstances, your modem will be in auto-answer mode only when you are there to see that the fax machine doesn't answer first.

If you have to go away and leave the modem in auto-answer mode, set the modem so it answers in fewer rings than the fax machine. Better yet, get a fax modem and let it determine which kind of call is incoming and it will respond appropriately.

Call Waiting

Call Waiting is bad news for modem transmissions. When your modem hears that little beep, it will usually interpret it as a sign to disconnect. So you'll need to disable Call Waiting before every modem call.

In most locations, Call Waiting is disabled by entering the sequence *70 before dialing the number (**1170** if you don't have touch-tone service). This will turn off Call Waiting for the duration of the current call. Most communications programs allow you to make this sequence automatic.

Using Two Lines

A better solution, particularly if you have a home business or make a lot of modem calls, is to get a second phone line. That line can be dedicated to fax and modem calls so your friends and/or customers can still get through even while you're online.

A second phone line will probably cost about $100 to install, plus whatever the monthly charge is in your area.

 TIP

For a home office, use the first line for incoming voice calls, both personal and business. Reserve the second line for faxes, modem calls, and outgoing business calls. That way you can keep your business expenses segregated for tax purposes as well.

A Final Note

Thinking through what you need in order for your modem to work well with your computer and on your phone system is, admittedly, not the glamour part of telecommunications. But like most preparatory work, it can save you a lot of grief down the road.

In the next chapter, we'll talk about spending money: where to spend it, how much you'll need to spend, and how to get the most for that money.

Three

Buying Your Modem

• •

Now that you have an idea what you want to buy, you need to know what you can expect to pay as well as where you're likely to get the best deal. Later in this chapter, we'll touch on what it'll cost you to actually use your modem.

The first rule to understand in buying a modem is that no one pays "list price." List price is of interest only to show where a modem is priced relative to others of a similar type. Your mission is to get the price as far "under list" as you can.

Before you even venture out into the cold cruel world, do as much research as you can bear. Buy a few computer magazines and look at the ads. In any given month, at least one of the major magazines will have a story about the lastest and greatest in modems. Look for those and read them. Ask your friends—if you have any (that use a modem, that is).

All the major manufacturers make good modems. Asking around and doing a little reading can help you avoid the occasional lemon (which even the best manufacturers seem to come up with once in a while).

Where's the Best Place to Buy?

What's the difference between a can of name-brand tuna bought at Gaspard's Gourmet Shoppe and an identical one bought at Dan's Dirt-Cheap Warehouse Foods?

If you answered, "About 65¢," then you grasp the difference among the various places to buy modems.

You'll pay more for a convenient location in a nice mall (maybe not so important) and for salespeople who know what they're selling (somewhat more important). Of course the nice convenient location may not have any people who know anything. On the other hand, the best technical people may be available only over the phone. There are lots of choices and trade-offs. It all depends on what it takes to maintain your comfort level.

Buying by Mail

The absolute cheapest way to buy a modem (or any other computer part) is by mail. It may sound scary, but in fact it's no more risky than buying in a local store.

If you've decided exactly what you want and have narrowed the choices to one or two models, mail order is ideal. Pick up a copy of *PC Magazine* or *PC Computing* and look at the mail order ads. For the ultimate in mail order, buy an issue of *Computer Shopper* (though considering its heft, this may result in information overload). Advertisers in these mainstream publications usually give fast and reliable service. Read the fine print about shipping costs and return policies, though—just to be on the safe side. Note that the outfits with the very lowest prices will not provide much in the way of technical support. In that case, if you're not able to get the modem working, your only option may be to return the modem.

Seven Rules for Mail Order Success

If you're looking through the ads and you see some that look promising—maybe even too good to be true—review the rules here to help you weed out the marginal companies.

1. Buy only from companies that include their full address somewhere in the advertisement. A place known by a P.O. box alone can be hard to track down in the event of a problem.

2. Look for sellers that have an 800 number for technical support. Almost everybody has an 800 number for orders because that *makes* them money, but tech support *costs* the seller money and that's where they tend to get stingy. An 800 number for tech support indicates that they'd like to make you a repeat customer.

3. Get an unconditional, 30-day (or longer) money-back guarantee. A phrase like "Satisfaction Guaranteed" is meaningless. You want to be able to get a *refund* (not a credit to buy something else from the same outfit) if the deal doesn't work out.

4. Beware of "restocking fees." That means they can charge you 10 or 15 percent just to take the darn thing back!

5. Buy from a place that warranties the merchandise directly. You want to deal with them, not the manufacturer, if you have a problem with the merchandise.

6. *Always read the fine print.*

7. Use your head. If most places are selling the modem you want for $200 and one outfit has it for $100, be suspicious—read Rules 1 through 6 (above) again.

On the other hand, some mail order companies do provide phone help. Two of them, with extensive catalogs and great prices, are PC Connection (800-800-5555) and MicroWarehouse (800-367-7080). PC Connection's claims to fame include toll-free technical support and overnight shipping for $5. MicroWarehouse offers a bulletin board where you can download information and ask questions of the technical staff, and cheap shipping. Both provide first-rate customer service in addition to technical support.

The disadvantages of mail order include that you'll have to package up and return something you've decided not to keep, and that you just may not be comfortable not being able to look that salesperson in the eye.

Buying at a Chain Store

Most urban and suburban areas will have one or more office or computer superstores like Office Max or CompUSA. These stores can often give you a price almost as good as the best mail order price—plus they will often have very good return and exchange policies.

The nice thing about these stores is that you can get what you want today and if it turns out *not* to be what you want, you can return it tomorrow. The disadvantage is that there may not be anyone at the store who has a clue about modems, so if you need help with your selection, you'll have to look elsewhere.

Buying at an Independent Computer Store

If you're not feeling the least bit adventurous, you may want to investigate a local computer store. Here's where you're likely to find a real live human who can answer questions. You can even bring your computer in and let *them* install the modem.

Don't be put off if the store seems to cater to business customers. Usually, they'll be quite pleased to sell you a modem, and they'll also have someone around the place who's knowledgeable.

Even here you shouldn't be paying list price. Your price won't be as low as that available by mail, but having someone with expertise nearby may compensate for the difference.

What Will I Have to Pay?

A few years ago, a 9600bps modem was a real bargain at $500. Today that same modem (plus fax capability) sells for about $175. What's even more interesting is that a fax modem that transmits 50 percent faster (in other words, at 14,400bps) can be bought for only $25 more!

These days, prices for both 9600bps and 14,400bps modems start at under $200 and go up to $500 or more. (This includes fax capability.) You can expect an internal modem to be about $10-$20 less than the identical external model.

Read the fine print carefully if you're offered a high-speed fax modem for much under $200. It may have limitations you won't want to live with.

What Comes in the Package?

Modems—particularly internal modems—are not very large, and yet they come in very large packages. Part of the extra stuff is packing material and other fluff included to ease your pain at parting with $250 plus tax, but inside all that, you'll find important stuff as well.

Documentation

Inside the box, along with the modem itself, you'll find some documentation, probably in the form of an installation guide and one or more user manuals. These manuals are not known for their clarity (or wit) but you will need to use them and keep them for future reference.

Unless you are the reckless sort of person who considers bungee jumping to be the ideal weekend amusement, don't accept a modem without full documentation, including a warranty registration card. Even a modem that's already installed can have problems in the future. Solving these problems usually requires referring to the documentation, and if you don't have the documentation, the odds of problems happening rise to 100 percent.

Warranty

Most modems come with long warranties—five or even seven years in covered time. The manufacturers offer these long warranties because it costs them very little to do so. This is because, like most solid-state devices, if a modem works when you first set it up, it's likely to continue working for a very long time. In other words, any manufacturing defect will show up in the first 30 days (if not the first 30 minutes).

As long as the modem is under some sort of warranty, it's OK. Under no circumstances should you pay extra for an extended warranty. It's a waste of money. Besides, you'll probably be replacing the modem with a better, faster modem long before a five-year warranty expires.

Software Included!

All modems will come with some communications software to help you get online. If it's a fax modem, there'll also be some software to use for faxing.

Your getting sleepy... sleeepy...

The advertisement may imply that ProComm or Crosstalk or some other communications package is included. In almost all cases, unfortunately, that software is a "stunted" version of the full ProComm or Crosstalk package. It will give you only limited functionality. Sometimes it's the fax software that's minimal. For example, you'll be able to send faxes but not receive them.

This is not to say that the included software is useless, it's just not usually all it's touted to be. It may show you enough so that you'll decide to buy the full package.

Bundled Software

If you look around, you can often find a real bargain in bundled software—packages of hardware and software wherein two or more products usually sold separately are "bundled" together. Usually the bundled software is a communications or fax package. This is not the truncated version included in the box, but the genuine full package that the retailer (or mail order company) will throw in when you buy a particular modem. Sometimes it'll be a financial package or a membership in an on-line service. Take care not to be dazzled in that case by the "savings." It's only a bargain if it's the modem *and the software* you want anyway.

Operating Costs

The initial purchase price is, of course, only the beginning of your investment. When you use a modem, you pay for the use of the phone line and, in many cases, for the use of an on-line service.

If you live in a metropolitan area, the phone company's charges will probably not amount to a lot. Most of the on-line services will have a local number in your area. But in many parts of the country, a "fast" line (i.e., one that lets you operate at 9600bps or 14,400bps) may be a toll call. Under those circumstances, you may want to use different numbers for different kinds of operations.

The on-line services also usually have different charges for different modem speeds. Everything up to 2400bps may be charged at one rate,while for 9600bps a premium may be charged. For example, the CompuServe information service (like many others) charges a flat monthly rate for its basic services and an hourly surcharge for so-called "extended services." Using the extended services at speeds up to 2400bps will cost $8 per hour. If you sign on at 9600bps or 14,400bps, it'll cost you $16 per hour.

Which is a better deal? That depends on what you're doing. If you're just pottering around online, reading the news or participating in an on-line conference (where the participants are all discussing some subject live-and-in-person), there's no need to operate at a fast speed. In that case, you'd want to sign on at the slowest speed possible, using a local phone number.

On the other hand, if you're downloading a file, you'll want to move as quickly as possible. A file transfer at 14,400bps will be seven times the speed of one at 2400bps, at only two times the cost. Under these circumstances, even paying a toll for using a more distant telephone connection can still save you money overall.

Here's an example. Let's say the nearest phone number where you can sign on at 9600bps is in the next county and costs 10¢ a minute to use. Your local sign-on number at 2400bps costs 5¢ a minute to use (now these are just examples, boys and girls, I don't know how things are where you live). The 9600bps number costs twice as much to use, but it transmits data four times as fast. So a file that costs 20¢ to download over the 2400bps number, costs just 10¢ over the 9600bps number. Of course, if it's CompuServe or some other service that charges more for 9600bps service, you have to factor that in, too! And, while it may sound like dimes and nickels now, these charges can really add up quickly.

I don't want to make things sound overly complicated, because most of the time it's pretty easy to figure out what's best for your situation, though it may take a bit of trial and error. In the sections on various on-line services, you'll find specific information on how to keep more of your money at home.

A Final Note

Selecting a place from which to buy a modem depends a lot on how much you want to pay for things that don't come in the box—technical support, a conveniently nearby store, and the comfort of being able to examine lots of modems in their boxes in person. The best assurance that you'll get a good deal comes from shopping around, reading a lot of advertisements, and asking friends about their experiences.

From here, we'll move on to installing the modem and making that first exciting connection to the outside world.

Part Two

Installing the Hardware and Software

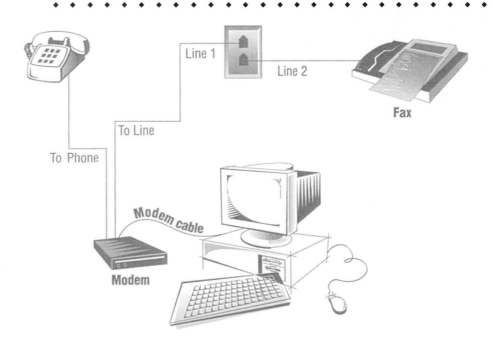

Line 1

Line 2

Fax

To Line

To Phone

Modem cable

Modem

Four

Installing an External Modem

• •

An external modem is easier to install by far than an internal modem. It does have a few more wires to deal with, but the actual installation is simplicity itself.

In spite of this, you should give at least a passing glance to the manual. Some (though not many) external modems have *switches* that need to be set. If yours is one of them, find out now, so you can have them properly set before you begin. Consult the manual to be sure.

When you install your modem, give some thought to where to place it in your work area. A modem needs at least *some* ventilation, so it shouldn't be tucked away under papers or in a very tight space. Position your modem so it won't be used as a resting place for other objects. You shouldn't be tempted to use your modem as a coaster for your soda glass, for example. A spill could very well be fatal to your modem.

Before you do anything to your computer, turn it off! It is hazardous to your computing health to plug anything into a computer while it's on. Better yet, unplug the computer at the power end (either the wall socket or the surge protector), so you can't accidentally start it up as you fumble around with the modem connections.

What You'll Need

In addition to the modem itself, you'll need:

- A phone cable with those little springy connectors at each end (otherwise known as RJ-11 connectors)
- A cable to connect the modem to the COM (serial) port on your computer
- A power cable (that probably includes one of those heavy transformer boxes)

The first and third of these items undoubtedly came with the modem when you bought it. Note that you can easily substitute your own phone connector if the wire supplied is not long enough. The second item might have come with the modem, though you can buy a cable separately.

Connecting the Phone Cable

On the back of your modem you'll find two places to plug in a phone line. The usual marking is one called "phone" and one called "line."

Plug the wire that came with the modem into the plug marked "line" and the other end into the wall jack. Plug your actual telephone into the socket on the modem called "phone." Then you'll be connected, as shown in Figure 4.1.

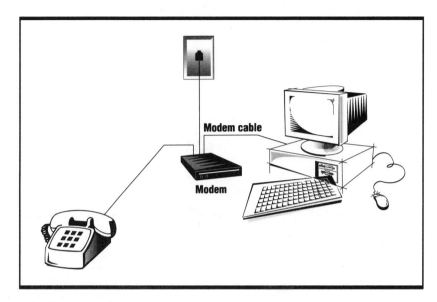

Figure 4.1

The most common way to hook up a phone and modem when there's just one phone line

If you don't want to plug your phone into the modem, use one of those line splitters shown in Figure 2.4 in Chapter 2.

If you have two phone lines, you can set things up as shown in Figure 4.2 or Figure 4.3. Using one of these setups, you can accommodate a variety of equipment.

 **WARNING**

You probably know that a surge protector is valuable protection for your computer. But big surges can also come your way via the phone line and they may fry your modem even if it isn't on. So plug your modem's phone line into a surge protector. A second phone line can go from the surge protector to the wall jack.

Figure 4.2

With the phone connected to line 1 and the modem connected to line 2, you can still use the phone while the modem is online or faxing.

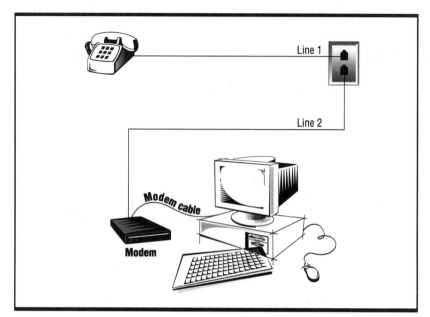

Figure 4.3

You can plug the phone and modem into line 1 and save line 2 as a dedicated line for incoming faxes. If you've got a fax modem you can still use it on line 1 for outgoing faxes.

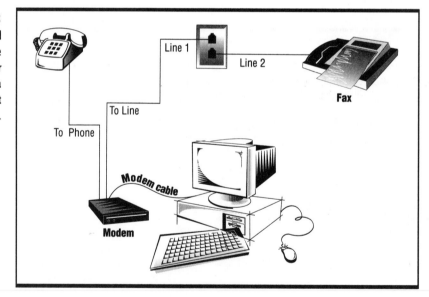

Connecting the Modem to the Computer

Your modem may have come with a serial cable to connect the modem to the computer. If it didn't, you'll need to buy one—probably at the same place you bought the modem.

Just ask for a *modem* cable—but check your computer first, to see if you need a DB-9 or a DB-25 connector at the computer end.

If your computer's serial ports (COM1 and COM2) have nine-pin connectors, you can use the cable that came with the modem as is. Just plug one end into the connector on the modem and the other into the nine-pin connector on the computer.

If your available COM port has a 25-pin connector, use the adapter that came with the modem. It has nine male pins on one side and 25 female pins on the other.

Make the connections secure by tightening the screws on the connectors. Tighten just to the point where the connections are snug. If you use too much torque you can damage the pins.

Getting Power

Plug the modem's power cable (or the transformer plug) into an electrical outlet. Better yet, plug it into the surge protector you use to keep your computer from frying in the next electrical storm.

A Final Note

The process of installing an external modem is so simple, it shouldn't take more than a few minutes. Your next step will be to turn your computer back on, install the software (Chapter 6) and see if everything works.

 **WARNING**

If your modem has a power switch, use it to turn the modem on and off rather than plugging and unplugging the modem's power supply. Plugging and unplugging the power supply can cause power surges, current overload, and other unpleasant consequences.

Five

Installing an Internal Modem

• •

Installing an internal modem sounds vaguely like some uncomfortable medical procedure, but it is relatively simple and usually painless. If you've installed a circuit board or two in your computer, you'll already know how easy it is.

Read the manual, though, because you will undoubtedly have to do something to the modem *before* you install it, and the manual will tell you what that is.

Setting the Modem Up

When you take your modem out of the box, it'll be sealed in a plastic protective pouch. Once you remove it from the plastic, handle it carefully and only by the edges. You shouldn't touch anything on the board itself, except any switches or jumpers that you need to set. In particular, *don't touch the edge of the board that has the metal connectors.* It won't ruin anything if you touch it, but the salts on your fingers can interfere with the electrical connection.

Somewhere on your modem there will be switches or jumpers of some sort that will need to be set. With any luck at all, these will be DIP switches that either slide up and down or rock back and forth. Figure 5.1 shows two of the common types of DIP switches.

The modem's documentation will tell you how to set the switches to various combinations—which you use will depend on what COM port you'll be using. As explained in Chapter 2 ("Getting More Ports"), this is where things can get a bit untidy. It all depends on what you already have on your computer.

NOTE

If you are very fortunate and have bought a modem from the right manufacturer, you won't have to set anything. The manual will advise you of this pleasant fact and you can just proceed to the section of this book titled "Popping the Hood."

Figure 5.1

DIP ("dual inline package") switches

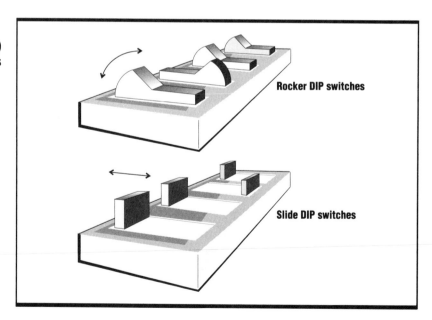

Rocker DIP switches

Slide DIP switches

If You Have One COM Port in Use

If you have a mouse on COM1, you can install your modem on COM2 or COM4. If COM1 is being used by some device other than a mouse, you can use COM3 if you won't ever be using the modem and whatever's on COM1 at the same time.

But if you have a mouse on COM1, you can't put anything on COM3 because the mouse is being used more or less all the time.

Confused? Take a look at Table 5.1, where you'll find a list of the possible COM port and IRQ combinations.

COM Port	Interrupt
COM1	IRQ4
COM2	IRQ3
COM3	IRQ4
COM4	IRQ3
COM3	IRQ5
COM4	IRQ2

Table 5.1
Possible COM port and IRQ combinations

The key thing to remember about IRQs (interrupts) is that an IRQ can only control one device, so don't try to use the same IRQ for two devices unless they absolutely, positively will never both be in action at the same time.

The easiest choice of the two (COM2 or COM4) is to use COM4. This is because you'd have to disable COM2 inside your computer in order to let the internal modem use it. If you're game to try it, go find your computer's documentation and look for the stuff on serial ports. It should tell you what to move on the serial board to disable COM2.

This is not so grim as it sounds. I recently had to do this on my own computer and I couldn't find a thing in the documentation about how to do it. So I just pulled out the circuit board into which my serial mouse was plugged. On the board were a series of pins with a plastic jumper, like you'll see in Figure 5.2.

 NOTE

The advantage of using COM2 is that all communications software will recognize it. But if you can't figure out how to disable COM2 so you can use it for your modem, go for COM4. Everything will probably work fine.

High-Tech Serial Ports

If you're doing your high-speed data transmissions in DOS, you only need to worry about having a 16550 UART in order to assure reliable performace. However, if you're trying to do the same thing in Windows and run your communications software in the background, you can end up with a sluggish performance as well as actual data loss.

Of course, those madcap hardware developers have come to the rescue with new and better (and more expensive) serial cards—generally called "intelligent" cards. These boards will let you select from a number of different IRQs and include their own processor on board, so you can do reliable communications (including faxing) in the background and never have to stop doing your other work.

An expensive version ($299) is the DigiBoard 2Port made by Digi-Board in Eden Prairie, Minnesota. A more modestly priced (and of course less fancy) version is the $99 T/Port made by Telcor Systems in Natick, Massachusetts.

But don't rush out to buy one of these intelligent cards until you're sure you need one. Your computer may well be able to handle all the demands you place on it without adding anything.

Figure 5.2

With a set of pins like this, you have only four possible settings, so I tried all four.

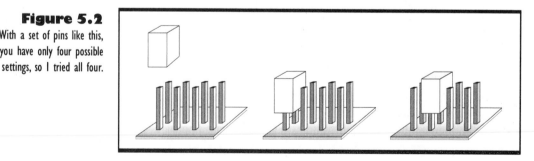

I just moved the jumper to the next set of pins, plugged the board back in and turned the computer on. When it booted up, I watched the screen to see which COM ports were enabled. I repeated the process until the screen told me only COM1 was there. At that point I skipped straight to "Putting the Modem Board in Its Place," a step you'll find described later in this chapter.

If You Have Two COM Ports in Use

If you're already using COM1 and COM2, you'll need to use one of the last four combinations in Table 5.1. You can use IRQ3 or IRQ4 only if the other device using that IRQ won't be in use at the same time as the modem. In other words, you can probably share an IRQ with a scanner as long as you're sure not to try to use the scanner while you're sending or receiving a fax.

Use of IRQ5 and IRQ2 is possible as a last resort. (Some old communications programs wouldn't let you use these IRQs, but that shouldn't be a problem today.) You do have to make sure that these IRQs aren't being used by something else, but this isn't very likely unless you have two printers, because IRQ5 is used by the second printer port, LPT2. Even then you can share the IRQ, as long as you're careful not to use the modem and the printer attached to LPT2 at the same time.

A Sample Solution

Let's say you already have two devices attached to serial ports, a mouse and a serial printer, and you want to add your new fax modem. You could set up the COM ports this way:

Mouse	COM1	IRQ4
Printer	COM2	IRQ3
Modem	COM4	IRQ3

In this example, the modem and printer can share an IRQ because most serial printer applications don't use the serial device's IRQ.

Another Sample Solution

Now let's say you already have a mouse, and a network board that's set up to use IRQ3, and you want to add your new modem. You could set things up this way:

Mouse	COM1	IRQ4
Network board		IRQ3
Modem	COM3	IRQ5

This of course assumes that you don't have some device actively using LPT2 (the secondary printer port).

 TIP

If you change the interrupt on your network board, you'll probably need to run a configuration program to let the network software know of the change.

Another solution would be to change the network board's interrupt to IRQ5. This is probably a bit better, because you could set up the modem to a more-standard COM2 that all communications programs can recognize. Then you'd have things set up as:

Mouse	COM1	IRQ4
Network board		IRQ5
Modem	COM2	IRQ3

As you can see, the more devices you attach to your computer the more crowded and complex things become. And sometimes some juggling as well as some compromises are required.

Popping the Hood

Once you have the switches set on your modem, it's time to open up the computer. You'll need one or two screwdrivers. Almost certainly one will have to be a Phillips screwdriver—the kind with the x-shaped head.

WARNING

Right now you're convinced you'll remember where everything plugs in. But when you're through with this process, you won't remember a thing! So go ahead and label all the cables and ports.

You'll also need a bit of room. If you have plenty of space on your desktop, you can work there. Otherwise you can put the computer on the floor or on a table.

First, turn the computer off completely. Then disconnect all the cables that are now attached to the computer. Label each one as to where it goes—you know, "monitor," "keyboard," etc. Put little bits of sticky labels next to the corresponding port on the computer box, labeled "monitor," and so forth.

Usually, getting inside a computer box is only a matter of removing some screws and sliding the cover off. In some cases, the documentation that came with your computer may be helpful, but generally, you just have to stare at the darn thing until you figure out which screws are holding the cover on. You want to remove the screws that are actually holding on the cover, but leave alone the ones that are securing the internal power supply in place. Figure 5.3 shows the usual way a PC cover comes off.

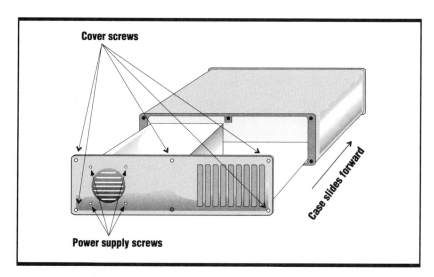

Cover screws

Power supply screws

Case slides forward

Figure 5.3

Just remove the screws and slide off the cover.

Remove the screws and put them where they won't fall down a heat register or into a crack and disappear. You'll need those screws to put humpty-dumpty back together again when you're finished.

Once you have the cover off, you'll see one or more circuit boards that are installed in slots. Slots look like black plastic furrows lined with metal; there will be several in your computer. Look for one that's the same length as the metal-covered tab on your modem card (which you are handling carefully by its edges). You can use one that's longer, but not one that's shorter.

More about Slots

Slots on your computer's motherboard can be in three different sizes: 8-bit, 16-bit, or 32-bit. The larger two have correspondingly longer connecting strips. Always try to use a slot that's the same size as the connector strip on the board you're installing. You *can* install an 8-bit card in a 16-bit slot, but you'll just be complicating things later (when you want to install a 16-bit card and don't have a slot available).

Putting the Modem in Its Place

Once you've found the slot you want to use, remove its backplate (see Figure 5.4). The backplate is the long, narrow piece of metal that keeps the dust out of the computer when a slot is empty. You need to remove the backplate so the part of the modem board where the phone line plugs in can stick out of the back of the computer.

 **WARNING**

Don't succumb to the temptation to use a magnetized screwdriver. Magnets should be kept away from computers, because magnets can easily erase data.

The backplate is held on with just one screw. Be careful not to drop the screw down into the computer's innards. Put the screw with the other screws you took off the back of the computer. You can save the backplate in case you ever want to remove the modem, but it's kind of pointless because you're bound to lose it long before then.

Position the modem board over the slot and slide the side with the metallic tabs into the slot as shown in Figure 5.5. It'll be a tight fit, so you may have to seesaw the board back and forth to get it in. If it doesn't go in with a moderate amount of pressure, pull it out and review the situation. Something may be blocking access (like a cable) and if you force it, you could break something expensive.

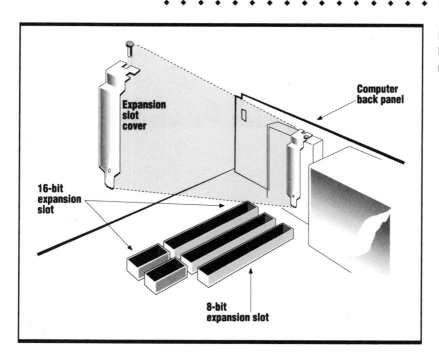

Figure 5.4
Remove the backplate to make room for your modem.

Expansion slot cover

Computer back panel

16-bit expansion slot

8-bit expansion slot

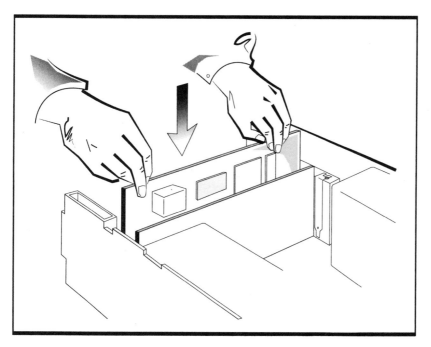

Figure 5.5
Touch only the edges of the modem board while you gently but firmly push it into the slot.

Use the same screw that came off the backplate to hold the modem in place. If the screw doesn't want to go in the obvious connection point, you may not have the modem board seated correctly.

Connecting the Phone Lines

On the part of your modem visible from the back of the computer, there will be two places to connect phone lines. One will be marked "Line" or "To Line." Plug one end of the phone line here and the other end to the phone jack in the wall (or in your surge protector). The other connection spot will be labeled "Phone" or "To Phone." You can plug your phone in here if you want. Figure 5.6 shows how the connection will look.

If you don't want to plug your phone in here, you can get a single-line splitter (shown in Figure 2.4, Chapter 2) and plug your phone in at the wall, too.

Figure 5.6

Making the phone and modem connections

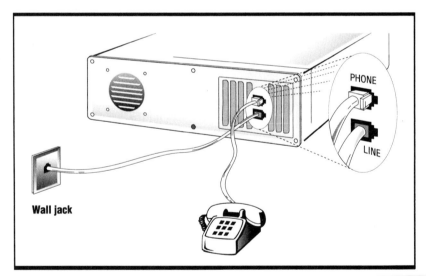

A Final Note

Whether or not to put the cover back on your computer at this point depends, again, on your comfort level. Most techie types will plug everything back in (leaving the cover off) and test everything to be sure it works. This way, they don't have to dismantle the whole thing again if the modem turns out to be nonfunctional for one reason or another.

You may feel too squeamish to leave everything so exposed—and besides, it's very likely to work on the first try, so go ahead and put the cover back on.

Reconnect the cables, connect the power cord and turn the computer back on. Now you can go to Chapter 6 to install the software and get going.

Six

Getting Started with Software

E verything on a computer has a hardware part and a software part. A modem or fax modem is no exception. Once you have the hardware—your modem—installed, you need to install the relevant software for your modem to actually do anything.

In this chapter I'll go over the minimum you need to know to get online (to make a first call), and what to look for in the software you might be looking to buy.

Is the Software in the Box Enough?

All modems come with some sort of software included. Usually the software is a stripped-down version of a bigger commercial package. For a fax modem, you'll usually get some fax software, too. Read the modem's package carefully—you may be getting software that will allow you to receive faxes but not send them (or vice versa).

Getting this sort of software is not necessarily a bad thing. If the modem you want comes with only a "teaser" version of software, it'll give you an opportunity to take a look at the package, try it out and decide later if you want to buy the full version. On the other hand, if the modem you want comes with a full package it may or may not be one you'll like.

A lot depends on how you plan to use the modem. If you plan to use CompuServe or Prodigy or another major on-line service most often, you'll want the software for that particular service. (Sometimes even *that* will come in the box.) In that case, even the most minimal communications program that comes with the modem will do fine. If you later want to do other things, you can then buy a bigger program.

On the other hand, if you plan to use your modem to transfer files, sign on to lots of different bulletin boards, or prowl the highways and byways of the Internet, you'll probably want the full version of a communications program such as ProComm or Crosstalk. These programs allow you to set up directories of different places you call, and configure each one to suit you. In any case, you might as well start out with whatever software is provided, so you can see if it has a look and feel that you like.

Many of the communications programs included with modems are DOS-based. This is not ideal if you tend to use Windows most of the time. Such programs will run in a DOS window inside Windows, but you may have a problem if all the following are true:

- Your modem is external
- You have an older UART on your serial port (see "How Great UART" in Chapter 1)
- You're doing high-speed data transfers
- You're running that DOS communications program in a window inside Windows

Having said all that, I must add that you may not have any problem at all. In fact, don't worry about any of this until and unless something goes wrong—the problems are not catastrophic when they do happen. You *may* find that some characters are dropped when you do a high-speed transfer, for example. If that happens, you might have to transmit the file again at a lower speed.

The surefire way to avoid this difficulty is to either buy yourself a new serial port with an updated UART or get yourself a Windows-based communications program.

Taking a Shortcut

If you're really only interested in CompuServe, America Online, or Prodigy, skip all this for now. Go straight to the chapter where your interest lies. For the most part, there are very easy, specialized programs for getting to these services.

It's true that you can use the "communications" program that came with your modem to call CompuServe, for example, but it's not an easy or pretty way to do it. You'll waste a lot of time and an alarming amount of money futzing around that way. Software that is made for CompuServe is a much more intelligent way to start.

In other cases—for example, Prodigy and America Online—there's no *there* there, unless you use the software provided by the service. There's simply no other way in.

Fax Software

If you're buying a fax modem to send and receive lots of faxes, the software in the box may not be enough, but it probably will be enough to get started (as long as it allows you to both send and receive).

Intel SatisFaxtion modems come with their own, very easy-to-use program called Faxability Plus. If you need to be able to convert faxes into editable files for your word processor or spreadsheet, however, you'll need the version with OCR (optical character recognition) capability—and that's only in the Faxability Plus/OCR, which is decidedly *not* included.

The specialized fax packages such as WinFax Pro and Eclipse come with OCR as well as a long list of fax management and manipulation tools. See Chapter 15 for more on fax software.

Installing the Software

No matter what the software is, it'll all install in pretty much the same way. Just follow the instructions on the pack or in the book(let) that comes with the disks.

My modem came with a program called Crosstalk Communicator, which is sort of the "lite" version of the DOS-based Crosstalk Mark IV. It's pretty typical of the kind of software that's supplied with most modems. In other words, it's definitely not friendly-looking, as you can see in Figure 6.1. (The documentation is even more hair-raising.)

 NOTE

If you're using dedicated software for Prodigy, America Online, or CompuServe (CIM or WinCIM), you don't need to know much beyond the speed of your modem and the phone number you're calling.

Even though I don't use the communications program a lot, I very quickly figured out that I wanted a Windows-based package—but no matter whether you use DOS or Windows, there's more weird language that you'll need to know.

Your software will probably have the ability to call the software manufacturer's BBS already built in. So you may be able to make that first call to the outside world just following the directions in the software or its documentation.

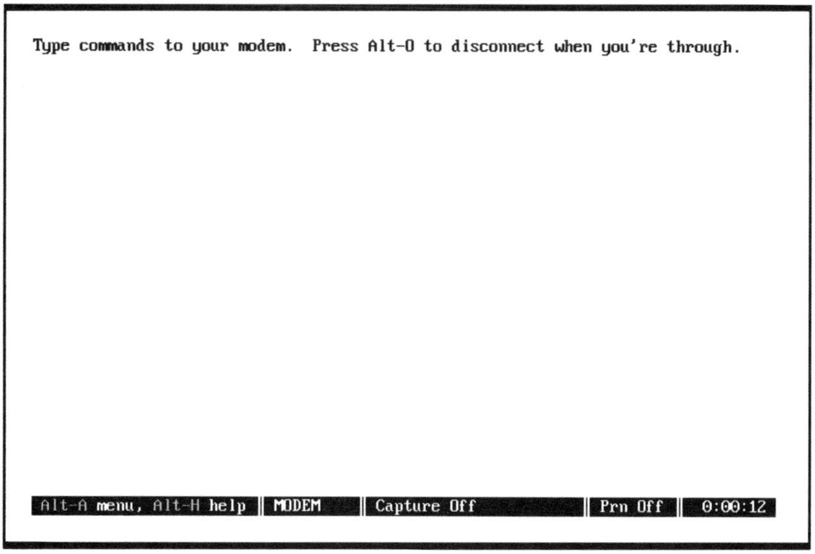

```
┌─────────────────────────────────────────────────────────────┐
│  Type commands to your modem.  Press Alt-O to disconnect when you're through. │
│                                                               │
│                                                               │
│                                                               │
│                                                               │
│                                                               │
│                                                               │
│                                                               │
│                                                               │
│                                                               │
│                                                               │
│                                                               │
│                                                               │
│                                                               │
│                                                               │
│ Alt-A menu, Alt-H help ║ MODEM ║  Capture Off    ║ Prn Off ║ 0:00:12 │
└─────────────────────────────────────────────────────────────┘
```

Figure 6.1

This screen from Crosstalk Communicator is not my idea of helpful.

Nevertheless, you may be asked to supply some information beyond that of the phone number you want to call. Here, in brief, are some of the terms you may need to know about.

Terminal Emulation

Terminal emulation just means the ability of your computer to make itself look like a terminal to another computer, such as the mainframes that operate CompuServe. All software will have some sort of terminal emulation available. The nice ones keep the whole process invisible to you.

Occasionally, you'll be asked to use a particular terminal emulation "for best results" but even then it's possible to make do with whatever you have available.

The basic terminal emulations are:

TTY	A generic mode supported by every monitor and every system
ANSI-BBS	A mode used by a lot of bulletin board systems
VT50, VT100, VT220	A mode originally designed for the terminals made by Digital Equipment, but used by lots of others now

If your software supports the above terminal emulations you're unlikely ever to need any others. However, if you know you're going to have to be calling a *lot* of different types of machines, the more emulations available in the software, the better.

Protocols

A *protocol* is a set of rules that determine the flow of data and how it's used. The modems at either end of a communication line have to be using the same protocol to talk to each other.

NOTE

If you're using the specific software made for America Online, Prodigy, or CompuServe, you don't have to worry about protocols. The necessary information is already written into the software.

Lots of different protocols have been developed over the years, usually with the intention of getting better speed and error correction. The most common are:

XMODEM	was developed in the late 70s. It's a dinosaur (too slow) but it's kept around because *everybody* recognizes XMODEM.
YMODEM	is faster than XMODEM, but is not so good on noisy phone lines.
Kermit	has to be mentioned because of its cute name. It's a useful protocol but only active on some systems.
ZMODEM	is the protocol of choice when you're given a choice. It's very common and has the best combination of speed and error-correcting abilities.

NOTE

For lots more on protocols, see Chapter 13, "Sending and Receiving Files."

Your software may well be smart enough to figure out the necessary protocol on its own, so you may not even be asked to supply this information. If it's not, you'll probably be successful using ZMODEM. If all else fails, try XMODEM because it's basically ubiquitous.

Data Bits, Stop Bits, Parity

These are other settings that are usually taken care of by the software. The settings are almost always *8 data bits, 1 stop bit* and *no parity* (usually abbreviated as 8,1,N or 8N1). ...*Almost* always, that is. Sometimes they'll be 7 data bits, 1 stop bit, and no parity.

Don't change whatever the default is in your software unless you are specifically instructed to do so (to reach a particular bulletin board or on-line service, for example).

These settings are just to make sure the data is transmitted correctly, and you don't need to know anything about what data bits, stop bits, and parity actually are unless you want to become a telecommunications guru (in which case, you need a different book).

Testing the Modem

The first time you actually complete a modem phone call is a real landmark. Let's step through the process using Terminal, the communications program that comes with Windows.

Terminal is actually a very modest (in other words, limited) package that has a lot in common with the kind of DOS-based programs that are supplied with many new modems. As you can see in Figure 6.2, the initial Terminal screen doesn't look any more helpful than the Crosstalk Communicator screen shown earlier in the chapter. It does, however, have all its functions available on easy-to-access menus.

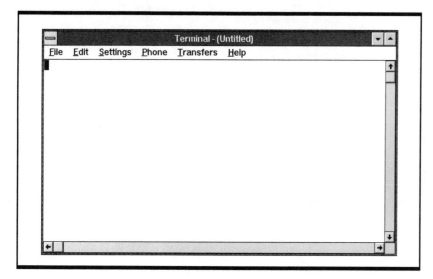

Figure 6.2
The initial (and unencouraging) Terminal screen

TIP

If you have an external modem, don't forget to turn it on. Many inexplicable modem problems come back to the fact that the modem was not switched to ON.

Your first step is to select Communications from the Settings menu. The first screen will look like Figure 6.3. As soon as you click on the COM port where your modem is installed, it lights up to look like Figure 6.4.

Figure 6.3

Your first look at the Communications settings

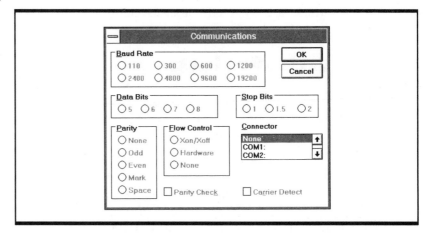

Figure 6.4

Select a COM port and the settings pop into place.

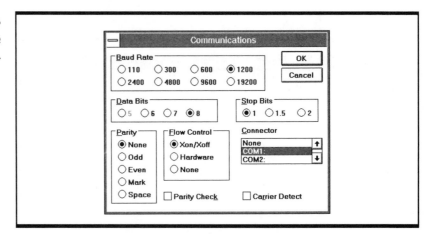

The only setting you should change is the Baud rate. Click on the Baud rate setting you know your modem can manage. Click on OK when you're done.

As soon as you do that, you can type AT and press the Enter key. The modem should reply OK as shown in Figure 6.5.

AT is the most basic command of the Hayes command set and stands for ATtention. If you don't get the OK, check that all the cables are plugged in correctly and securely, and make sure that when you were in Settings ➤ Communications, you checked the correct port. For example, you may have the modem in COM2 while the program is trying to talk to COM1.

 NOTE

You can always run your modem at a slower rate than its maximum, but if you overstate the speed, it won't work. You also have to be sure not to overstate the rate at which the modem at the **other** end can send and receive.

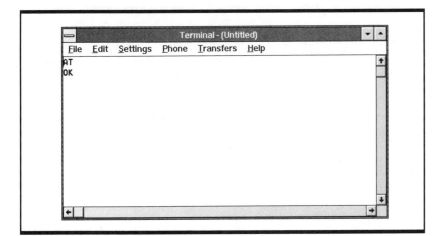

Figure 6.5
You speak and the modem speaks back.

You can look around at the other settings, but you're better off not changing them until and unless you're instructed to use different settings.

Making a Call

As a test, we can make a toll-free call to the information line maintained by DELPHI (an on-line service discussed in Chapter 10, "Exploring the Internet").

Select Phone Number from the Settings menu and type in the phone number shown in Figure 6.6. If you have Call Waiting, type *70, (including the comma) in front of the phone number. *70 disables Call Waiting for the duration of this call; the comma inserts enough of a pause for the disabling to take effect before the dialing starts.

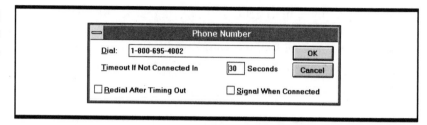

Click on OK. You'll hear the sounds of dialing, followed by ringing, followed by the most dreadful screeching and wailing. This, oddly enough, means you've been successful. The screen will look like Figure 6.7.

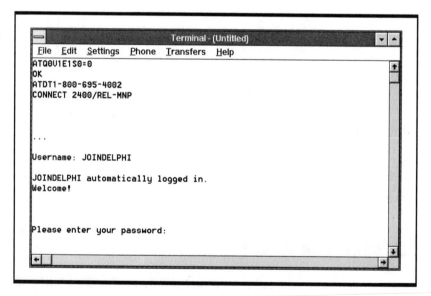

Press the Enter key. If nothing happens, press it again. In the space provided for a password, type **INFO** and press Enter again.

If you want the information, just follow the instructions on the screen. Otherwise, type **EXIT** and press the Enter key. The modem at the other end will disconnect and send instructions to do likewise to your modem. If for some reason this doesn't happen, just select Hangup from the Phone menu.

TIP

Try a lower baud rate if your connection doesn't seem to be working right.

Now that you've made a successful connection, you can try the bulletin board (BBS) of your modem's manufacturer (the number is in the documentation somewhere). Or go to the chapter of this book that covers the on-line service you're most interested in.

In the next part of this chapter, you'll find the pros and cons of some of the most widely used communications programs and why you want one of them instead of Terminal.

ProComm Plus for Windows

ProComm Plus for Windows is my first choice of communications packages because it's easy to use and yet it has just about all the features you'll ever need even if you turned into a modem-head of unimaginable proportions.

It's certainly not perfect, but ProComm Plus does have Dialing Directories that are pretty easy to figure out, and once you have one set up, you won't have to deal with it again until something changes.

Figure 6.8 shows the main screen of ProComm Plus for Windows. The program automatically sends a couple of commands to your modem. That's the code in the upper-left corner of the screen.

With ProComm, you mainly want to set up a Dialing Directory. Do that by clicking on the icon that looks like a book at the left end of the icon bar. This will open a Dialing Directory.

It's pretty simple—double-click on the name field, then enter the name of the person/service/bulletin board you want to call. Press Tab and you're at the phone number. Type in the full number, including any preliminary numbers such as *70 to disable Call Waiting or 9 to get an outside line.

Figure 6.8

The opening screen for ProComm for Windows

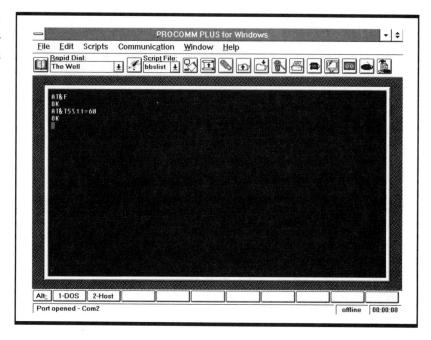

You don't have to enter any information (unless you want to) other than the name and number. Even using the default for the Baud rate setting will usually work. ProComm does a pretty good job of figuring out how to connect to the other end. Of course, if you *know* certain information to be important, just click once on the field and a menu will open allowing you to either choose an entry or type one in. A filled-in Dialing Directory is shown in Figure 6.9.

Figure 6.9

This is a completed Dialing Directory.

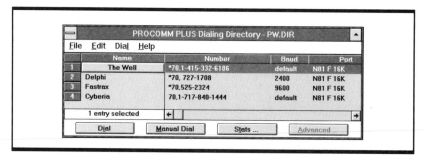

Once you have your directory information entered, save the directory as PW.DIR. Then whenever you enter ProComm you can just click on the Rapid Dial drop-down list, select the entry you want, and Pro-Comm will be off and dialing.

ProComm has a tool bar for the most common functions used online. It's probably as much as you'll ever need—at least until you become that real modem-head mentioned earlier.

ProComm Facts

ProComm for Windows sells for just under $100 in the catalogs. The list price is more like $150. (A DOS version costs about $25 less and is also very good but, of course, not quite as easy to figure out.)

You'll need, in addition to your modem and mouse,

- A computer that runs Microsoft Windows in Standard or Enhanced mode
- At least 2MB of available hard-drive space

Crosstalk

Although I'm no great fan of the DOS-based Crosstalk Communicator, Crosstalk for Windows is a lot easier to deal with, especially if you want to sign on to services for which the program has a ready-made setup.

Figure 6.10 shows the initial screen for Crosstalk. Just click on one of the selections and Crosstalk will step you through the process of getting to that service.

Crosstalk has quite a few predefined setups, including AT&T Mail, CompuServe, Delphi, Dialog, Dow-Jones, GEnie, Lexis, MCI Mail, Newsnet, and the Official Airline Guide.

After you've gone through a setup once, Crosstalk will, in the future, skip right to the process of getting you online without any input from you.

Crosstalk's weakness is in the area of getting to places that aren't part of the original system. Trying to set up an automated logon for a local bulletin board, for example, is an exercise in frustration. I suppose I could

Figure 6.10

The initial screen for Crosstalk
for Windows (version 2.0)

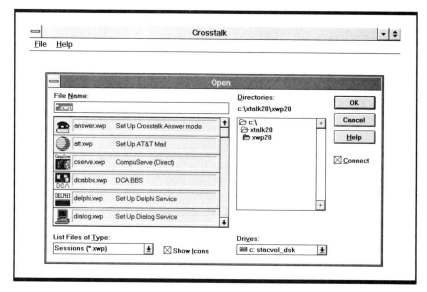

have gotten it to work, but the time and energy necessary would have been too extreme.

I tried really hard to like Crosstalk because all the ads tout the many awards it's won from magazines as their "Product of the Year" and some such. I figured I was just being dense at first. In the end, I decided that even though it's promoted as having a lot of advanced features, I hardly see the point if you can't get them to work without a whole lot of effort.

On the other hand, obviously lots of other people like Crosstalk. Maybe *you* will, too.

Crosstalk Facts

Crosstalk sells for about $100 in the catalogs and lists for close to $200 (another example of how ridiculous the so-called list prices are). In addition to your modem and a mouse, to use Crosstalk you'll need:

- A computer that runs Microsoft Windows in Standard or Enhanced mode
- At least 4MB of available hard-drive space

Microlink

Microlink is a good example of why shareware continues to survive and even thrive—if you can find it.

Microlink runs in Windows and has a very friendly look to it. In other words, you can potter around, push on-screen buttons, and figure out how to do most things. For the things you can't figure out that way, there's an extensive Help system that's actually helpful! Figure 6.11 shows the opening screen.

The good news is that Microlink is shareware. You can try it out without obligation. If you decide you like it, you can become a registered user for the very modest sum of $35 plus $4 shipping. Unfortunately, that's the bad news as well. It's not easy to order a copy of Microlink by phone. You can order by writing to MicroWerks, P.O. Box 768273, Roswell, GA 30076-73, or if you can get to CompuServe, you can send a message to Stephen Leitner at 72510,1766.

 NOTE

Shareware (such as MicroLink) is the original try-before-you-buy software. You get it from catalogs and bulletin boards. If you like the software and continue to use it, you're on your honor to send a registration fee to the software's designer/owner. The registration fee is usually quite small and entitles you to updates or extra features.

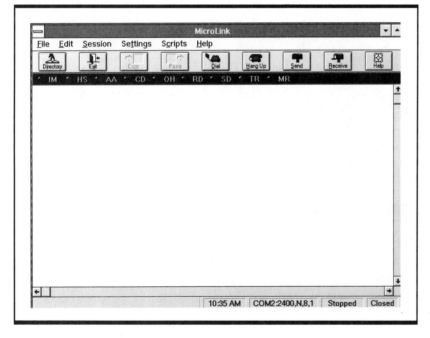

Figure 6.11
Microlink comes with the usual Windows menus and buttons.

It *is* worth the effort, though. You'll get a good program and the kind of friendly technical support that the big companies usually fail to provide.

Microlink Facts

Microlink is not only one of the cheapest Windows communications programs, it's also one of the smallest, taking up less than 1MB of hard-drive space. You will still need a computer running Windows 3.0 or later, and a mouse.

Other Communications Programs

There are of course lots of other communications programs—all of them with their own zealous fans and adherents. If someone promotes a particular program to you, try to get a look at it and ask lots of questions before you buy. Here's what I know and believe about some of the other major players.

Mirror

Mirror started out as a sort of clone of an earlier version of Crosstalk. It has lots of different looks to it and if you can find one you like, it works pretty well. Mirror III (the DOS version) allows you to send and receive faxes as well. Mirror for Windows (version 1.2) does not work nearly as well as the DOS variety. (Later editions may be more reliable.)

Smartcom

Smartcom is a good product if you have an honest-and-true actual modem made by the Hayes Corporation. That's because Hayes makes Smartcom, too, and they don't make it easy for you if you have a modem manufactured by someone else.

Smartcom is inexpensive (less than $50 in some catalogs) but it doesn't include any setups for the popular on-line services and it is very finicky when working with any modem other than those made by Hayes.

DynaComm

DynaComm has almost as many features as ProComm Plus and only costs twice as much. ...What can I say? At $249 list, it's one of the more expensive packages.

It does have a few more predefined setups for on-line services than ProComm, but fewer than Crosstalk or Mirror. It's a good program with lots of terminal emulations and protocols and the usual stuff, but it really doesn't have anything special to make it worth the higher price.

A Final Note

All the programs (as you can see) have strengths and weaknesses. In assessing them, you'll want to look at the following:

Compatibility	Will it run on your system?
Hard-disk space	Do you have enough room for it on your hard drive?
Script Language	How easy is the *script language*? Scripts are the communications version of macros. The program will supply some scripts, but you'll want to be able to write your own logon scripts to access particular services.
Terminal emulations	All programs will support the most common ones: ANSI, VT100 and TTY. If you're going to be communicating with lots of different computers, look for a package with the maximum number of terminal emulations.

Protocols	(Same as for terminal emulations.) You can probably use a modem for years without using anything besides ZMODEM. But if you're going to be communicating far and wide, the more protocols you have at your disposal, the better.
.GIF File Viewer	When you find a graphic file on a bulletin board, it'll almost always be in the .GIF format. Some programs include a built-in viewer so you can see the picture even while you're in the process of receiving it.

 Take a long, cool, appraising look at the software you got with your modem. You may find it to be quite enough for your purposes at this time—besides, the longer you wait to buy a "full" communications program, the better off you'll be, because these programs get easier and better in every new version.

Part Three

Getting Online

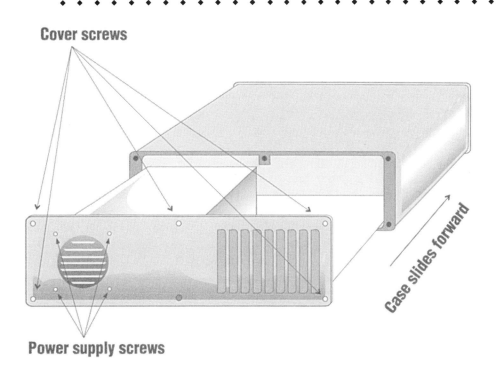

Cover screws

Power supply screws

Case slides forward

Seven

Prodigy

• •

Prodigy is a very big on-line service that advertises a lot in magazines and on radio and television. They're probably the best known and certainly the largest service available, reaching about a million households. Prodigy has been around for a number of years without generating a lot of excitement, but that's recently changed.

In July 1993, Prodigy raised its prices drastically and—as many subscribers concluded—unilaterally. The subscribers reacted predictably and left in droves (the primary beneficiary was America Online, which signed up thousands of Prodigy refugees). By the end of 1993, Prodigy began its counterattack, which included a new interface for DOS users, a new Mail Manager allowing Prodigy subscribers to become part of the larger world of e-mail for the first time, and a Prodigy for Windows program. Prodigy, which looked positively moribund in mid-1993, is back with a vengeance.

Prodigy's big selling points include lots of children's features and lots of news and entertainment features—it's sort of like television, only slightly more interactive. Prodigy resembles television in another way, too, in that there's an advertisement on virtually every screen. To be fair, some of the ads are for very interesting products, and some are for services that you might otherwise order by phone. Using the computer to order those services can make the whole process a great deal easier. On the other hand, the relentlessness of the advertising can get on one's nerves.

Prodigy is unique in allowing up to six persons to have personal IDs on a single account. That means that your kids can each have an account and sign on individually. Each person's account is private. You can keep the kids or other members on your account from running up excessive bills, though. See "What's It Cost?" later in this chapter for information on how to monitor and control the use of the account by subsidiary members.

You can get to Prodigy only by using Prodigy software, which you can buy in virtually any computer store or by calling 1-800-PRODIGY to order directly. Both DOS and Windows versions are available.

For most of its existence, Prodigy has been much more of a closed system than the other big services. You could send and receive mail among other Prodigy customers but that's it—you couldn't e-mail outside of the Prodigy system. At the end of 1993, though, Prodigy added a feature called the Mail Manager, so you can now send mail to almost anyone (who has a computer and a modem) almost anywhere in the world. There's more on sending mail of all kinds under "Using the Mail Manager" later in this chapter.

Prodigy looks very different from most of the popular services. The screens are bright and colorful with lots of graphics. Some places, notably in the shopping mall, have photos and sound attached. This is nice but means that if you have to access Prodigy at 2400bps, it's so slow you'll want to scream. Fortunately, you *can* access Prodigy at 9600bps and, unlike some on-line services, Prodigy charges nothing extra for the faster speed.

What'll I Find There?

Prodigy is a pretty crowded place. It's wide, but you have to make an effort to go very deep.

The news and sports coverage is updated constantly but tends to be the computer equivalent of the ten-second sound bite. The daily features are fairly shallow in general, but it is possible to get a lot more information than is apparent on the surface.

For example, there is an on-line encyclopedia and a number of services—particularly in the areas of investing and business—that provide considerable detail. Guest "columnists" are featured regularly, with articles presented in each of their fields of expertise, which range from movies to politics to wines and beyond. Once you learn your way around you can set a path for yourself to visit regularly the areas that interest you.

The coverage for kids is excellent, ranging from "Sesame Street" features to rock 'n roll news. The children's areas are updated constantly and tend toward the educational, cleverly disguised as the entertaining.

Installing the Software

For a long time, Prodigy was available only in a DOS version. The software did its best to *look* like Windows, but without a lot of success. Now Prodigy is available in a Windows version—and it's very attractive, too. If you use Windows at all, get the Windows version. Not only is it better looking, it installs much more easily and reliably.

The Prodigy software comes in a box with several small manuals, containing a member guide, a member ID, and a temporary password. Keep all this stuff nearby during the installation and enrollment process because you will need to refer to most of it at one time or another.

Installing the Windows Software

To install the Prodigy Windows software, put the floppy disk in drive A:. Select Run from the Program Manager's File menu and type **INSTALL** in the Command Line box. Click on OK.

The software will let you know where it has located your modem (what COM port) and then pretty much proceed to install itself. When it's finished, you'll have a new group window that looks like Figure 7.1.

Upgrading to Windows from DOS

If you have the DOS version of Prodigy already installed, upgrading to the Windows software is very easy. Just start Prodigy in the usual way and Jump to Windows Upgrade. Then follow the instructions to download the software.

After the download is completed, exit Prodigy. When you're back at a DOS prompt, make a new directory called PRODTEMP and copy the downloaded file (called PRODWIN.EXE) to it. Make the PRODTEMP directory your current directory and type **PRODWIN**. This will cause the self-extracting PRODWIN.EXE file to decompress. When it's finished, you should have a whole bunch of files in the PRODTEMP directory.

Now you need to start Windows and select Run from the Program Manager's File Menu. Type:

```
c:\PRODTEMP\INSTALL
```

in the Command Line box and click on OK. After that, just follow the prompts.

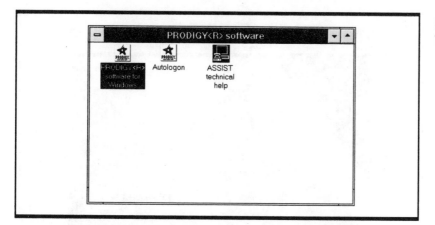

Figure 7.1
The Prodigy group window

Getting Online with Prodigy for Windows

Click on the icon with the label "Prodigy<R> software for Windows" to get started. You can use the Autologon icon only after you've gone through the enrollment process and become a member. When you get the sign-on window, you'll need to find the member ID and temporary password that came with your startup kit.

Type them in the appropriate boxes, as shown in Figure 7.2.

You'll be asked some questions about your modem's maximum speed and your phone, then the software will dial an 800 number. At the other end is the Prodigy phone directory. The software will step you through the process of picking the right phone numbers for your location.

When you're through picking phone numbers, you're ready to sign on. The screen prompts will show you how.

 NOTE

When you type in a password in Prodigy, it appears on screen as "*****" (just in case your dog is watching and he's always wanted a chance to run up your on-line bill). This allows you to keep the password a secret.

Figure 7.2

The Prodigy sign-on screen

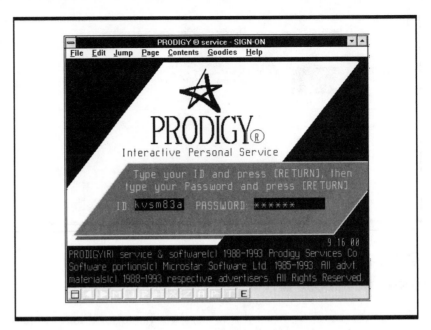

Installing the DOS Software

The DOS software is a model of the easy-to-install variety, though there are one or two possible pitfalls. You'll have to provide more information, for example, about your printer setup, video, and so forth.

If your A: drive is the $3\frac{1}{2}$-inch size, you'll just have one disk. For an A: drive of the $5\frac{1}{4}$-inch size, there'll be two disks.

To install the software, start your computer. Once it's sitting at the C: prompt, put the Prodigy disk in the A: drive, type **A:INSTALL** and press the Enter key. If you have a printer connected to your computer, make sure it's switched on.

Do read the screens as they go by. The program is very good at making intelligent guesses about your system, but it's not perfect. You'll want to be able to change anything that isn't correct as you go along. First you'll get a screen showing what the software knows and what it doesn't. Then you'll have to supply whatever is missing, as shown in Figure 7.3.

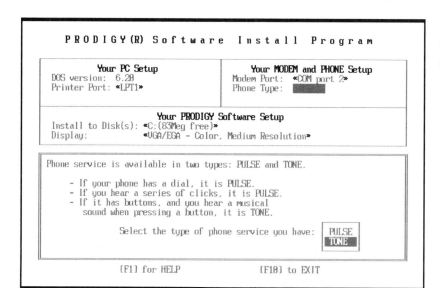

Figure 7.3

Prodigy can usually figure out everything except the phone type.

Then you'll get a chance to change any of the settings you know to be wrong. Proceed with caution, though. Don't change anything unless you're sure.

The next screen that appears, shown in Figure 7.4, asks if you want to allow the software to use more disk space to run faster. You should answer Yes unless your hard disk is extremely crowded. The total amount of space is very small (only about 1.5MB); in return you'll get faster operation.

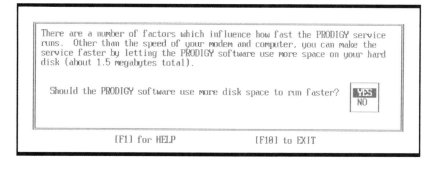

Figure 7.4

Answer Yes to get a noticeably faster operation.

If You Have Trouble

If the installation hangs your computer in mid-process, you may have a problem that's easily fixed. Restart your computer with a boot floppy in drive A:. Or, if you have DOS 6 or higher, press the F5 key as soon as you see the Starting MS-DOS prompt. *Now* run the Install program. This often works for reasons that I don't understand (nor do the Prodigy support people). It probably has something to do with device drivers or resident programs that the Prodigy software takes a mysterious dislike to.

You may have another problem if you're fortunate enough to have a very large hard disk (more than 500MB). In that case, the Prodigy software will not install directly. You'll have to follow the procedure to install the software to a floppy disk. After you've done that, you can copy the installed files from the floppy to your hard disk.

The software is now copied over to your hard disk. Don't forget to read those screens! When the whole process is done, you'll be back at the DOS prompt, but inside the Prodigy directory.

Getting Online with Prodigy for DOS

 NOTE

When you install the DOS software, the program puts a file called PRODIGY.BAT in the root directory of your hard disk. This means that Prodigy will start whenever you type **PRODIGY** at a DOS prompt without the Prodigy directory being placed on your path.

Now all you have to do is type **PRODIGY** at the DOS prompt and press Enter. You'll get the Prodigy screen (you can see it in Figure 7.5), which provides a place to type in your member ID and password—both these bits of information are in the Prodigy startup kit. The ID number will stay with you as long as you have Prodigy, but the password provided by Prodigy is strictly temporary. You'll soon get an opportunity to change it to one you like better.

Type in the ID, press the Tab key, and then type in the password. Press Enter and then go look for the Prodigy Phone Book that also came in your startup kit.

Figure 7.5
The Prodigy startup screen in DOS

If you can't find a number nearby, you can call 1-800-PRODIGY for a newer list of numbers. You can also sign on with the nearest number you can find and then select Phone Numbers from the About PRODIGY menu to get updated listings.

You'll want two phone numbers from the Prodigy Phone Book: one primary number and one for when the primary number is busy or not in service (this secondary number is not required). Look in the book for the number that's geographically closest to you—in other words, the one that's not a toll call.

If the number you choose has a network symbol of Q, you're supposed to get your secondary number from the gray pages in the back of the phone book. If the number you choose as your primary number has the network symbol Y, just choose the next closest location as your secondary number, regardless of whether it's a Q or a Y.

Type in the numbers as if you were dialing them yourself. (You can include hyphens, but it's not required.) Don't include the area code as part of the number if you're calling within your area code.

 NOTE
If you're upgrading from the DOS version of Prodigy to the Windows version, you don't have to worry about this stuff. The Windows software finds your password, your ID number, and the telephone numbers you're already using, and plugs them in to the new software.

 NOTE
Don't forget any necessary prefixes, such as *70 to disable Call Waiting on a tone phone. If you use a prefix, it should be followed by a comma to insert a pause before the number is dialed.

A Few Words about Telephone Networks

All on-line services are run by mainframe computers somewhere. Prodigy's computers are in White Plains, New York, and America Online is run from Virginia. So, sadly, it can't be a local phone call for everyone.

The on-line services deal with this by using telephone networks that most people don't even know exist. That's because these networks, known as packet-switching networks, are usually used by businesses. But in the world of on-line services the various networks loom large. The networks are what make it possible for you to make a local telephone call and connect with a computer in a distant city without paying long distance rates.

The major public packet-switching networks are SprintNet and TymNet. Both of them are very large, with phone numbers in hundreds of cities and thousands of phone exchanges. Private packet-switching networks are also owned by CompuServe and Prodigy, among others.

When you use the specialized front-end software for Prodigy or CompuServe or America Online, the connection to the packet-switching network is done for you without fuss or muss. However, if you get involved with bulletin boards or smaller services in distant cities, you may need to call a public packet-switching network directly. The bulletin board will be able to provide you with detailed instructions on how to do so.

You'll have to choose a modem speed. The only choices are 1200 or 2400bps. If you have a modem that can send and receive at 9600bps, you have to do the setup for that speed online. Choose 2400 for now.

As soon as you press Enter, the program goes to work, dialing the primary number. Once a connection is made, the computer at Prodigy has a discussion with your computer about the software and then any changes that have been made in the software since your installation disks were manufactured are processed. In a couple of minutes, you'll get the Welcome screen and you're ready to enroll.

Enrolling

Just follow the instructions on the screen. You'll provide the information they need to bill you. They're careful to let you know which information is optional, too. At this point you can select your own password in place of XZ&VBF or #BF4SD or whatever temporary password you have.

Once you're through enrolling you'll get the Welcome New Member screen shown in Figure 7.6.

 NOTE

If you have any trouble with installation or setup, Prodigy provides very good technical support at 1-800-PRODIGY. The people are helpful, friendly, and willing to spend as much time with you as necessary.

Figure 7.6
You've arrived!

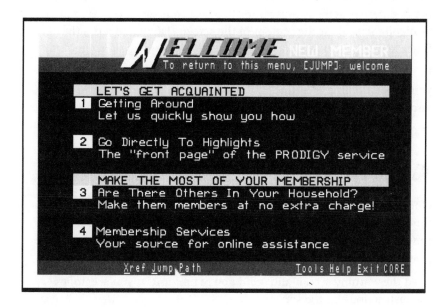

Do select the Getting Around option. Getting Around is a quick tour through Prodigy's features and navigational tools. It only takes a few minutes and will give you a good introduction to the service.

Getting 9600bps Service in DOS

The Windows version of the software will give you a 9600bps option before you sign on. With the DOS software, you have to sign up for a slower speed (2400bps) and then go online and make the change there.

Select Jump from the bottom of the screen and type:

> 9600 SETUP

You'll be stepped through the process of getting a 9600bps phone number and configuring the Prodigy software to run at 9600bps.

Having It Your Way

The Prodigy software is relatively flexible, so you can configure a number of different items to suit yourself. Select Jump ➤ Tools (Windows) or highlight Tools at the bottom of the screen (DOS) and press the Enter key.

From the Tools menu, you can find out your latest usage, how long you've been online this time, and lots of other information. You can also change some basic settings such as your password, the colors of some displays, and your printing options.

Autologon

One of the handiest items in the Tool menu is AUTOLOGON. This function eliminates the need to type in that dorky member ID every time you sign on. You can automate only the ID or both the ID and the password.

Read the warning screen and see if you're up for it. If you are, follow the instructions on the screen.

Shopping Cards

Plan to do a bit of spending in the on-line mall? This is where you enter credit card information that will allow you to spend more money than you ever intended. (If you *do* enter information here, you'll now have an excellent reason for keeping your password a secret.)

Change Display

If you're running the DOS software and have a VGA monitor, you may be able to improve the look of Prodigy considerably. Choose the Change Display option and Prodigy will step you through a process that can make the Prodigy screen both sharper and brighter-looking. If you're using Windows, you're automatically getting the best display from the first time you sign on.

Change High, Change Path

After you've explored for a while, you'll know what areas are of interest to you. The Change High and Change Path options let you select the initial Highlights screen that appears when you sign on and customize your Path so you can visit the same areas in each session.

Using the Mail Manager

To send e-mail to people outside the Prodigy system (or to receive it), you'll need a program called the Mail Manager. It doesn't currently come with the Prodigy software, so you have to get online and download it. This is not difficult, because Prodigy will figuratively hold your hand through the whole process.

You'll need to start Prodigy, and once you're connected, Jump Mail Manager and follow the prompts. After you download the program, exit Prodigy and go to the directory where the program was downloaded (probably the PRODIGY directory). Print out the installation information by typing:

    COPY READ.ME PRN

The instructions in this file cover installation for both DOS and Windows users. After installation is complete, you can also print out any of the Help files by selecting the Print button at the bottom of any Help window.

Mail Manager is pretty easy to use at a basic level. Table 7.1 shows the type of mail you can send. In addition, Mail Manager includes a lot of advanced features that you can either approach gingerly or ignore completely. Consult the Help files for assistance.

Table 7.1

Mail Manager messages and their size limits

Message Type	Maximum Size	Real-World Equivalent
Prodigy e-mail	60,000 characters	About 20 pages
E-mail outside Prodigy	60,000 characters	About 20 pages
Prodigy fax	20 pages	20 pages
Prodigy postal letter	4 pages	4 pages
Prodigy file transfer	1,048,576 bytes	1 Megabyte

The pricing structure for using Mail Manager is described in the "What's It Cost?" section later in this chapter.

Basic Principles of Navigation

When you first become a member of Prodigy, you move around primarily through the use of "Jump" words. Jump is almost always an option at the bottom of every screen. Click on Jump (or J in Windows) and then type in the name of the destination. If you don't know the exact name of the destination, click on A-Z at the bottom of the screen to get the full index of services and the associated Jump words.

When the A-Z screen comes up (Figure 7.7), you'll get the first page of an index for the whole system. Special interest A-Z listings are attached to the buttons on the right of the screen.

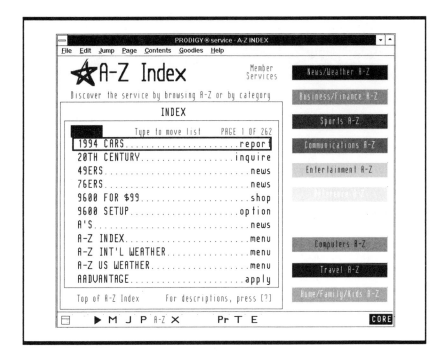

Figure 7.7

The A-Z index screen is a good place to start your exploration of Prodigy.

Deciphering the Tool Bar/Command Bar

The row of buttons at the bottom of the screen is called a Tool Bar in the Windows software (Figure 7.8) and a Command Bar in the DOS software. The buttons in both versions of the software work in very similar ways. The only difference is that you can customize the Tool Bar in the Windows version (select Goodies ➤ Tool Bar Setup).

Table 7.2 shows what each default button does. Not all the buttons are available on all screens.

Figure 7.8

The Tool Bar in Prodigy for Windows

Table 7.2

Tool Bar/Command Bar functions

Windows button	DOS Button	What It Does
▤	▤	Return to Highlights screen
◄	◄	Move to previous page
►	►	Move to next page
J	Jump	Go directly to selected location
M	Menu	Move to top of section
P	Path	Move to next step on path (Prodigy provides a default path, but you can set up your own)
A-Z	A-Z	Go to full index of services
X	X-Ref	Go to related topic
Pr	C	Print screen
T	Tools	Open Tools menu
A		Signals action when ordering or making a purchase
Z	Zip	Return to original screen (after you have selected LOOK in an advertisement)
	?	Go to Help (for help in Windows, select Help Hub from the Prodigy Help menu)
E	Exit	Leave Prodigy

What's It Cost?

Most of the on-line services seem to have unnecessarily complicated pricing policies, and Prodigy is certainly the champion in that regard. Until July 1993, Prodigy charged a flat rate per account and that was that. Now there are four plans (see Table 7.3), each of which has a different approach to the four types of things you can be looking at in Prodigy.

Free features are unexciting things such as membership changes, billing inquiries and getting information about Prodigy itself. But shopping in the mall and using the on-line banks are also free. When you're doing free stuff, there's a FREE sign in the lower-right corner of your screen.

Core features are news, sports, weather, and entertainment. You'll get a box that says CORE in the lower-right corner of the screen when you're in a Core area.

Plus features are the bulletin boards, QUOTE CHECK/QUOTE TRACK (investing information), and EAASY SABRE (the airline reservation service). The box in the lower-right corner of your screen will change to PLUS when you're in one of those areas.

Extra Fees features are the special ones, such as Strategic Investor and "Write to Washington" letters. You'll get fair warning when you enter one of these areas. The box in the lower-right corner of your screen will show four asterisks(****).

Table 7.3 shows what each plan offers and what it costs.

Table 7.3

Prodigy plans and prices

Plan Name	Price per Month	How Many Free Hours?	How Many Free E-Mail Messages?	How Much for Extra Hours?	How Much for Extra Messages?
Value	$14.95	Unlimited Core; 2 hours Plus	30	$3.60 each	$.25 each
Alternate	$ 7.95	2 hours Core and Plus combined	0	same	same
Alternate-#2	$19.95	8 hours Core and Plus combined	0	same	same
Alternate-BB	$29.95	25 hours Core and Plus combined	0	same	same

Mail Manager Fees

The pricing structure for sending and receiving mail is fairly complicated. However, for the simple sending and receiving of e-mail, it's not too difficult to figure out:

- Send e-mail and it'll cost you 10¢.
- Receive e-mail from someone not on the Prodigy system and it'll cost you 10¢.
- Send a file to someone on the Prodigy system and it'll cost you 10¢ for every 6,000 bytes.
- Send a fax via Prodigy and it will cost you $1.25 a page.
- Send a letter through the US Postal Service via Prodigy and it will cost $1.50 for up to four pages.

Things get complicated, though, if you start sending and receiving e-mail messages longer than about two pages or if you have a membership plan that includes a monthly allowance of messages. In that case, you should Jump Mail Manager and print out the fee schedule.

Saving Money on Prodigy

As a general rule, I'd advise signing on for the cheapest service. For exploring, the $7.95 per month Alternate Plan is as cheap as any. If, after a month or two, you find that you're sending a lot of mail or spending a fair amount of time online, you may want to switch to another plan, which is easily done. (Jump Membership Fees.)

All these prices are "per household." Prodigy does give you a chance to protect yourself from the marauding kids on your account by allowing the primary member to restrict use of the account. The person who first enrolls on the account becomes the primary member (and gets an ID number that ends in the letter "A").

Just go to the Tools list and select Member Access. There you can add other household members to your account and control their access to Plus features or specific bulletin boards.

You should also check out Bulletin Board Questions for the latest on how to use the bulletin boards economically. Prodigy's been making lots of changes in that area—ever since the Great Member Revolt of 1993.

Inside Story

The Prodigy software includes some valuable programs that are not immediately apparent. These programs can give you a lot of help with basic as well as more advanced topics. Go to the Prodigy subdirectory on your hard drive and type **INFORM** at the prompt.

Click on Troubleshooting Guide and you'll find out how to change the printer port, printer type, or graphics resolution. Also in this area are troubleshooting hints you can use if you're unable to install the software, unable to connect to the service, or having problems with memory-resident programs.

If you click on Advanced Topics, you'll get a screen like that in Figure 7.9. You can get some truly advanced information here, including technical stuff on how the service actually works behind the scenes.

Figure 7.9

Advanced topics covered in the Information Center

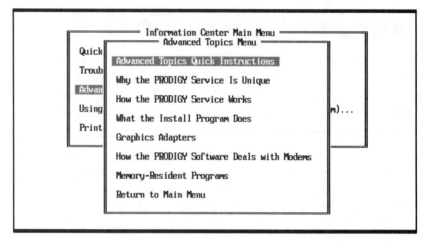

Also hidden away in the Prodigy subdirectory is a program called DI-AGNOSE. Type the name **DIAGNOSE** at the prompt and you'll get a program that can help you identify possible port conflicts and determine if your modem is properly communicating with the Prodigy software.

Windows users can get help with error codes by double-clicking on the Assist icon in the Prodigy group window. For problems other than error codes, exit Windows completely and go to the PRODIGY directory. Type **ASSIST** at the DOS prompt to get help with any problems that keep you from connecting to the service.

Utilities for Prodigy/DOS

A number of companies have come up with programs to make Prodigy/DOS easier to use, on the grounds that the Prodigy software is too clumsy and slow to use. The best of these is made by Pete Royston and can be downloaded directly off Prodigy.

Select Jump on any screen and Jump to ROYSTON. You can read all about the utilities there. The package, called Pro-Util, provides many functions missing from the Prodigy software, such as a spell checker, macros, and the ability to compose messages offline. Pro-Util will also let you change the screen colors, customize printing operations, set up your own address book, and do lots of other useful tricks.

You can order the utilities by mail or download them directly from Prodigy. The instructions for downloading are provided on screen and are very easy. The best part is that Pro-Util will cost you less than $30 (including shipping and/or sales tax if applicable). Pete Royston also provides good on-line technical support if you need help.

If you find yourself using Prodigy a lot, an investment in Pro-Util will pay for itself very quickly.

A Final Note

Prodigy is a good choice for people first starting out with computers and modems. It has a pretty interface and it's easy to use. When you make mistakes in Prodigy you won't get stuck in places or feel stymied. Their telephone support is among the best.

Prodigy is among the most fluid of the available on-line services. If you sign up for Prodigy and then don't sign on for a while, you'll find it dramatically changed when you do. New features and services are being added or changed almost weekly. Prodigy's reputation as a place where serious telecommunications don't go on is rapidly changing; it still maintains its feel as a fun place as well.

If you have kids who are interested in on-line services and playing around with computers, they'll like Prodigy, too. In fact, even if *you* get tired of the service, the kids may well stay interested for considerably longer.

Eight

CompuServe

. . . .

CompuServe has been around for a number of years and claims more than a million users worldwide, but until recently it was largely the province of nerdly types. This was because the software you had to use to get to CompuServe was notable mainly for its unfriendliness. It was hard to figure out where you were and where you wanted to go. That's all changed now; you can access CompuServe easily with programs designed specifically for that purpose.

CompuServe bills itself as the service you'll never outgrow. That's certainly true. In fact, the only down side to CompuServe is that you have to be careful or you'll run up a horrendous bill. You'll be in the poorhouse *long* before you outgrow it!

It's definitely possible, however, to use CompuServe economically. In this chapter we'll cover the best programs to use to learn about CompuServe and the best programs to use to save money.

What'll I Find There?

The basic services of CompuServe are pretty impressive. In addition to the usual news, weather, on-line encyclopedia, stock quotes, and electronic shopping, there are extras such as:

- Peterson's College Database
- U.S. Department of State travel advisories
- HealthNet, a medical reference source
- EAASY SABRE, the airline information and reservation service

all at no extra charges.

There's less emphasis at the basic level in CompuServe on entertainment and games than in Prodigy and there are far fewer features aimed at children. But CompuServe's strengths include more than 1700 databases you can use. Virtually every maker of computer hardware and software maintains some presence on CompuServe, so you can get answers to any computing problem you have. The special interest forums range all over the map and the reference library is unparalleled.

Almost all the really good stuff costs extra. Read "Saving Money on CompuServe" later in this chapter for advice you'll need if you plan to use this service very much.

Getting the Software

NOTE

Many general-purpose communications programs provide a script for use with CompuServe. This is not a good idea for beginners because the interface is unhelpful in the extreme. You're bound to find it frustrating and intimidating. Start with CIM or WinCIM. You can use either of them until you know your way around.

You should start your CompuServe adventure with one of the programs designed specifically for CompuServe access. The CompuServe Information Manager (known as CIM or DOS CIM) works in a DOS environment. WinCIM is made to run in Windows. Most of the examples in this chapter will be from WinCIM (because I think it's easier to use and looks better than DOS CIM).

You can order the software directly from CompuServe. Call 1-800-848-8199. DOS CIM and WinCIM each cost $25—they throw in $25 in usage credit after you join, though.

If you have a friend who already belongs to CompuServe, such a person could go to Membership services and order a membership kit for you. That will earn $25 in free usage for you and $25 in free usage for your friend.

Those in a great big hurry can run out to a software store and buy the full CompuServe startup kit for around $39.95. This also comes with the $25 credit for service after you join. If you do buy the full kit, check the box to be sure you're getting the latest version: for DOS it's version 2, for Windows it's version 1.1.

Installing the Software

Both CIM and WinCIM pretty much install themselves, which is a good thing, because the instructions that come with the software are not models of clarity.

For the DOS version, just put the first disk in the appropriate floppy drive. Change to that drive and type:

    INSTALL

then press Enter.

For WinCIM, start Windows, put the floppy in the drive, and select Run from the Program Manager's File menu. In the Command Line box, type:

    A:\SETUP.EXE

and click on the OK button (substitute B: for A: if the floppy is in your B: drive). The software will offer to install the program in a directory called CSERVE. Let it.

Next you'll be asked if you want to copy the Signup files. You'll need these in order to actually join CompuServe, so say Yes. You can read the Help screens as they go by, but they're mostly CompuServe puffery, so don't feel bad if you miss one.

Then you'll be asked if you want to sign up a new membership. Say Yes and go look for the identification numbers that came with your membership kit.

The next screen (shown in Figure 8.1) gives you a number of options. Before you actually sign up, you should probably read the service agreement and rules.

Then you should check the Connection Settings (as shown in Figure 8.2). They're probably correct, but the phone type may be wrong. Leave the Modem Settings alone. They're likely to be right. You can change them if you know for sure one or more of them is wrong.

Enrolling

NOTE

If you join CompuServe with some versions of CIM and WinCIM, or by using another communications program, you'll be asked instead for the Signup User ID Number and the Signup Password. These are also in the introductory subscription package.

Select Signup from the Signup menu. In the next screen (Figure 8.3) you'll need to type in the Agreement Number and Serial Number that you'll find lurking somewhere in the CompuServe materials.

You'll have to supply some information about yourself for the usual reasons—so they can bill you. In the selection of Membership Options, even if you don't want any of the others, do get the CompuServe Magazine. It doesn't cost extra and it's a great source for keeping you up-to-date on new features and changes in the system.

Figure 8.1

The Signup screen

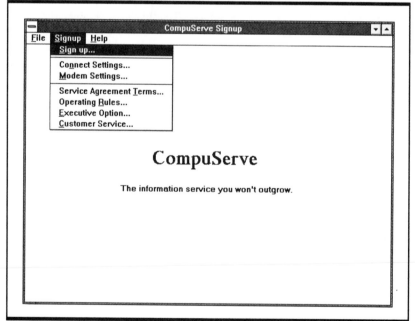

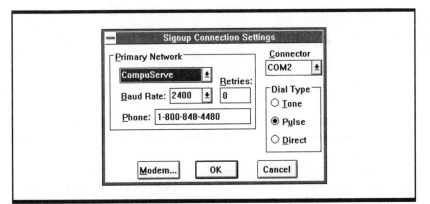

Figure 8.2
Check these connection settings to make sure they're correct. Don't change the phone number.

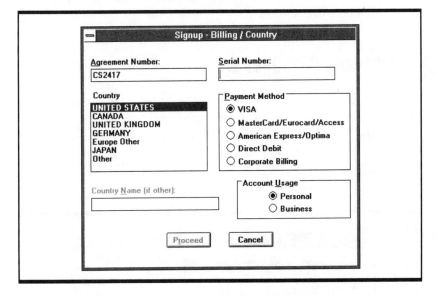

Figure 8.3
Type in the agreement number and serial number supplied with the CompuServe disks.

Keep going through the screens, supplying the information needed, and the program will dial CompuServe and sign you up as shown in Figure 8.4.

At the end of this process you'll be presented with a User ID, a password, and a local access phone number. Write all this stuff down and put it in a safe place. The program has already transferred this information to the Session Settings, but if your computer or software has a

Figure 8.4

The Signup information is transmitted to CompuServe.

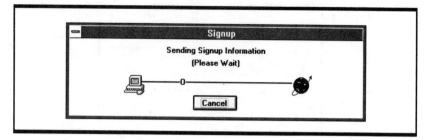

nervous breakdown, it's a nuisance to replace the information—particularly the password, because they have to send you a new one by mail.

In any case, this password is valid only until CompuServe sends you a new one in about ten days—a security measure to make sure you are who and where you say you are.

Getting Online

NOTE

In the CompuServe group window, you'll also find an icon for the CompuServe Directory. Look here to get a list of all the services available and descriptions of what they offer.

Getting to CompuServe is very simple with either CIM or WinCIM. You just start up the software, select the activity you want from a menu and let the program do the work. You can check how everything's set up by looking at the Session Settings under the Special menu, as shown in Figure 8.5.

Figure 8.5

This is the Session Settings dialog box in WinCIM 1.1.

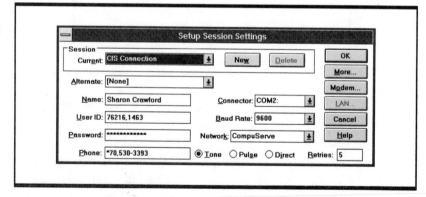

Fast Modem Speeds

CompuServe has phone numbers practically everywhere for modem speeds of 2400bps and below. 9600bps numbers are available in all urban and many suburban locations, though you may have to make a toll call to get to one.

Starting in the fall of 1993, CompuServe became the first major service to offer connections at 14.4Kbps. These connections are available only in about a dozen cities, but their number is expected to grow in the next year until they're as widely available as 9600bps connections.

Because different modem speeds incur different charges on Compu-Serve (see "What's It Cost?" later in this chapter), you need to develop different strategies for different kinds of use. Part of that strategy is whether the different modem connection points incur different phone connect charges.

For most people, the major expense involved in using CompuServe is incurred on line. The (usually) local phone calls don't add up to much, but your case could be different. You'll either have to consult with the local phone company or keep a close eye on the phone bill for the first month or so to make sure things aren't out of hand.

The potentially big expense in using CompuServe comes from spending time in forums and other extended or premium services. These charge by the hour, with the hourly rate based on the modem speed you're using.

If you have a fast modem and a choice of local numbers, you should tailor your speed to your use. For example, if you're downloading files or mail, 9600bps or 14.4Kbps is best because you want to spend as little time on line as possible. If, on the other hand, you're browsing in forums or poking around in a database, you're better off using 2400bps because you can't really read faster than that.

Some special interest forums hold chats or conferences online. If you want to join in on one of these discussions, sign on at 300bps because it's the cheapest possible rate and neither you nor anyone else in the discussion can type faster than 300bps.

 **NOTE**
For on-line conferencing, always sign on at the slowest rate that makes financial sense.

To make several sign-on options, look up the appropriate local phone numbers by selecting Go from the Service menu and typing **PHONES** in the Service text box.

After you've found the phone numbers for the different modem speeds you want to use, write them down and disconnect the phone connection. Then select Session Settings from the Special menu. Click on the New button and type in a name for this alternate connection, such as *CIS Conferences*. Type in the new phone number and select a new bps setting. Click on the OK button when you're finished.

Multiple settings are also handy if you travel a lot with your trusty laptop and modem. You can have a connection set for each city you visit. When you settle down again in one city, just use the Delete button to get rid of the ones you no longer want.

Having It Your Way

Setting up multiple sign-ons, as described above, is certainly part of having it your way. Another way to customize the setup is in the list of Favorite Places. You can open the Favorite Places dialog box by clicking on the rather loathsome pink heart icon on the button bar. You'll be surprised to see that the software has already picked out some "favorite" places *for* you, as shown in Figure 8.6.

See all those places marked FREE? All of them, except perhaps the Order from CompuServe, are must-haves. The Practice Forum is extremely useful, because you can potter around there to your heart's content without incurring a dime of on-line charges. The WinCIM Support Forum (CIM Support Forum for DOS CIM) is also free. If you have any problem with the software, this is the place to go for answers.

As you can see in Figure 8.6, you can easily make this list of favorite destinations into your own. After you've roamed about in CompuServe a bit, you can use the Add button to add an area to the list and you can use the Delete button to get rid of ones you don't want.

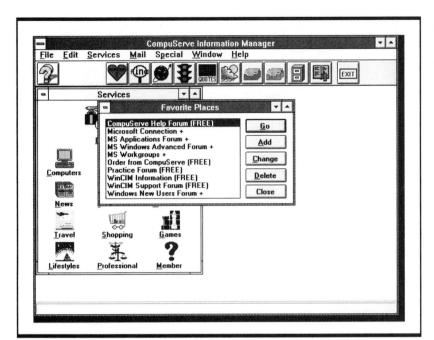

Figure 8.6
The default list of Favorite
Places

Basic Principles of Navigation

WinCIM is particularly easy to move around in. As shown in Figure 8.7, most of the functions pop up when you first open the program.

The Services window displays icons for all the major areas. Click on one of them and the software will connect you to that part of CompuServe.

The button bar at the top of the screen shows you shortcuts to specific operations.

 **NOTE**

In WinCIM 1.1, the button bar is configurable. Just select Special➤ Preferences➤Ribbon and you can change what's on the button bar.

Figure 8.7

The opening screen for WinCIM

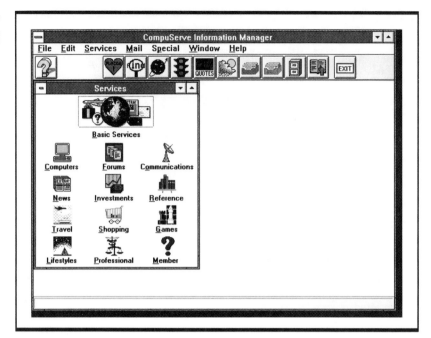

The list of your favorite spots (discussed earlier under "Having It Your Way") can be seen by clicking on the heart button:

To search for a particular topic, click on the Find button:

Type in a subject you want information on and click OK. The program will search through the system and find any places in CompuServe that might be what you're looking for. You can then pick from a list or search again for another topic.

The button with the globe on it:

will take you to the top level of the service (from wherever you are). This button only works when you're actually online.

If you know the name of a service and want to go directly there, click on this button:

For example, if you want to go to the Science and Math Education Forum, type **SCIENCE** in the Go dialog box.

To get a list of stock quotes, click on this button:

and a dialog box will open. In the dialog box you can add or delete ticker symbols and then get updated quotes at any time of day.

For an instant weather report, click on the button with the clouds:

You can then pick from a long list of locations for specific weather reports, or you can enter your own request either by state, country, or weather station.

The next button represents your In basket:

This is where the program stores your incoming mail messages, and where you can read, answer, file, or delete the messages.

This means, of course, that the next button is for the Out basket:

Here's where you store outgoing messages until you're ready to actually send them.

The next button opens up your file cabinet:

NOTE

If you don't want to keep copies of every outgoing message, select Special▶Preferences▶Mail, remove the X from the File Outgoing Messages box, then click on OK.

When you first start WinCIM, the filing cabinet has only two folders in it:

- Auto-Filed
- GENERAL

as shown in Figure 8.8. Auto-Filed is where copies of all your outgoing messages are stored and GENERAL is, well, general.

Figure 8.8

The Filing Cabinet when it's new

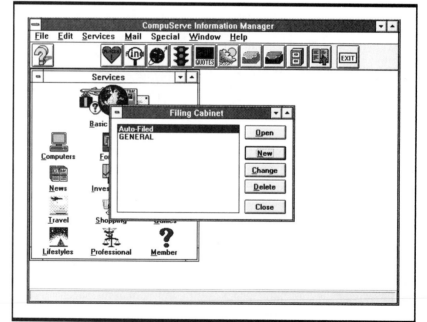

By clicking on the New button, you can easily add folders of your own devising to the list. Then you can stash your incoming mail in places that make sense to you.

The button that looks like a book:

represents your address book. It's completely empty when you first install WinCIM, but every time you select Mail▶Create New Mail, you get a chance to add the recipient to your address book.

The Exit button:

closes the WinCIM program.

When you're online, this button:

will appear on the button bar. Click on it to immediately disconnect from CompuServe and hang up the phone line.

Two other buttons can appear on the button bar when you're online. Click on this one:

and you'll immediately leave whatever service you're in.

The button with the mailbox:

tells you that you have mail waiting.

NOTE

When you're reading mail, you can click on any To or From button to add that person's name to your own address book.

For context-sensitive help, click on the button with the question mark:

The space between the Help button and the Favorite Places button, as shown in Figure 8.9, reports on how long you've been online. This is vital information when you're paying by the minute!

Figure 8.9
The report that tells you how long you've been online

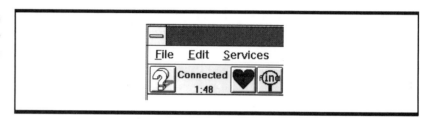

If you close WinCIM and reopen it, the connect time restarts at zero. However, if you shrink WinCIM to an icon even if you go on- and offline a number of times, the connect time is cumulative.

Check out the menus as well as the button bar. Use the free Practice Forum. It's an ideal place to get a feel for the system without pressure. You'll learn how to compose and send messages, use the forum libraries, send files, and download files. All these things are easy to do but you might find them a lot more difficult when you're in a regular forum and are aware that every minute is costing you money!

What's It Cost?

Essentially, there are two pricing plans for CompuServe. First is the Standard plan. For this one you pay $8.95 per month, get unlimited access to the basic features and pay extra only for the extended services. This is the plan you're automatically assigned to at Signup.

There's also an Alternative plan, for which you pay $2.50 per month and nothing's free. You pay for all connect time. Tables 8.1 and 8.2 show the billing rates.

Modem Speed (bps)	Price per hour
300	$ 6.00
1200,2400	$ 8.00
9600,14400	$16.00

Table 8.1

Standard plan's connect time rates

Modem Speed (bps)	Price per hour
300	$ 6.30
1200,2400	$12.80
9600,14400	$22.80

Table 8.2

Alternative plan's connect time rates

Remember that the Standard plan's connect rates apply only when you're in one of the extended services, which includes most of the forums. Connect time is billed in one-minute increments and doesn't include whatever you have to pay the phone company to get to CompuServe.

Saving Money on CompuServe

The secret to saving money on CompuServe is to do as much *offline* as possible. This means copying all your mail and forum messages to your In basket or File Cabinet and reading them when you're safely disconnected. Likewise, compose all your mail and replies to forum messages offline, keeping them in the Out basket until you're ready to go online and send them.

But if you're going to be spending any time at all on CompuServe using the extended services, you'll want to investigate one of the programs designed to get you on- and offline as quickly as possible. These programs are generally not good for exploring, because they require you to know exactly where you're going and what you want to do when you get there.

Two such programs (both downloadable off CompuServe) are TapCIS and OzCIS. Let's say you regularly want to visit the Literary Forum

(LITFORUM), get all the messages addressed to you specifically, and get all the newest discussion in the Mystery/Suspense section. You can set up either TapCIS or OzCIS to sign on to that forum, send any messages you've written to that forum, get your messages, and sign off—at dazzling speed.

Neither of these programs will win prizes for ease-of-use (OzCIS is better in that regard), but you can cut your on-line bill drastically. TapCIS has its own forum, which you can find by using the Go function on the Services menu or by clicking on the traffic light button. Type **TAPCIS** in the text box. To get OzCIS, use the Find button and type **OZCIS** in the text box. OzCIS has a download area as well as a library in the IBM Communications forum (IBMCOM).

Both products are shareware, which means you can use them for some specified period of time and then, if you want to continue, you'll need to pay a registration fee.

Inside Story

One WinCIM quirk is that it has a disturbing habit of occasionally "disappearing" your mail. That is, you'll write a message or receive a message and get the alarming message that WinCIM can't find the message. This is all the more baffling because the message appears to be right there! You can see the date, the subject, and who it's from (or who you addressed it to in the case of outgoing mail), but WinCIM refuses to see it.

Although scary, this is much more of a nuisance than a disaster. Select Special▶Rebuild Cabinet Indexes. You get a warning that this may take a long time, but it won't unless you have thousands of messages filed away. After it finishes the rebuild, look for your message again. You probably still won't be able to see it, but you'll feel better, having tried the less drastic solution.

If you still can't get at the message, exit WinCIM entirely, then go to the Windows File Manager and your CSERVE directory. You'll have to go down two levels to get to the CABINET subdirectory (C:\CSERVE\FCABINET\CABINET). In the CABINET subdirectory, delete *all* the files with the extension .IDX. ...That's right, delete them.

Then you can restart WinCIM, and all the indexes will be built *again*, except this time your message will be readable.

Another trivial but annoying thing is the About WinCIM box that pops up every time you open the program. To get rid of it, select Special▶Preferences▶General and remove the checkmark next to the About box under Initial Desktop.

A Final Note

CompuServe is a most amazing place. You can get every kind of information you can imagine and lots of stuff you never knew existed. Want access to the National Medical Library, which has 7 *million* medical journal articles on file? It's under PCH. How about the names, addresses, and phone numbers of over 75 million US households? You'll find that under PHONEFILE. The European Company Library —EUROLIB—has information on 2 million European businesses. You can get all this, for a price, and a lot more.

The forums alone are a veritable treasure chest. The most extensive technical support anywhere for computer hardware and software is available here. Whether you need information about cultural customs in Saudi Arabia, why Swiss cheese has holes in it, or solving a behavioral problem with your German Shepherd, you're likely to find someone who's not only knowledgeable, but generously willing to share their expertise with you—and the response may well come from Saudi Arabia, Switzerland, Germany, or any of fifty other countries around the world.

CompuServe can turn expensive very quickly, so unless your company is picking up the tab, you'll have to learn how to use the system to your best advantage. That might take some experimenting, or you might have to adopt a specialized program to save money. Once you find your way around CompuServe, however, you may find it to be an indispensable resource.

Nine

America Online

• •

America Online (AOL) is the number three on-line service in terms of total subscribers—right behind Prodigy and CompuServe. It's growing rapidly, however, having added more than 100,000 customers in the second half of 1993.

A goodly number of those new customers were Prodigy's loss. A lot of people fled Prodigy when their prices went up in July of 1993. In fact, so many users left Prodigy for America Online that AOL now has a Prodigy Refugee Message Center specifically for those new arrivals!

America Online is relatively cheap and has at least as many features, services, and forums as any other on-line service. On the down side, the organization of the files and forums is sometimes chaotic and difficult to understand. You'll easily use up all your free time figuring out where things are—at least, for the first month or two.

What'll I Find There?

America Online has all the features you expect from an on-line service:

- Technical support for computer hardware and software
- Travel information (including the ubiquitous EAASY Sabre)
- News, weather, stock quotes
- Entertainment and games
- Special interest forums

What distinguishes AOL from others is the emphasis on actual on-line, live participation. Much of the activity at America Online centers around "Chat rooms" where people (up to 23 at a time) have discussions on all kinds of subjects. Some of these are regularly scheduled, some spring up like mushrooms after a rainstorm (see "Basic Principles of Navigation" later in this chapter).

Getting the Software

America Online makes it pretty easy to get the software to access their service. Just call 1-800-827-6364 at any hour of the day or night. Even if no one's there, you can leave a message asking for the free software. They'll send it out to you right away.

The software comes in versions for DOS or Windows. They work almost identically, but the Windows version looks nicer.

Installing the Software

As with most programs, the Windows version of the software is less complicated to install than the DOS version. This is because AOL/Windows just looks at all the settings (for your printer, mouse, modem) in the Microsoft Windows files and copies those. This is information that the DOS program has to guess at or ask you for.

Windows Version

Installing the America Online software for Windows is simplicity itself. Just put the disk in the appropriate drive and select Run from the File menu in Program Manager. Type **A:INSTALL** in the Command Line box (substitute B: if the disk is in your B: drive) and click on OK.

The software installs itself with very little input from you. At the end of the process, you'll have a new Group window in which America Online resides in solitary splendor. Double-click on the America Online icon to proceed.

The first time you open America Online, you'll get a screen that resembles the one in Figure 9.1. If you see anything that doesn't look right, select the Other Options button to make changes.

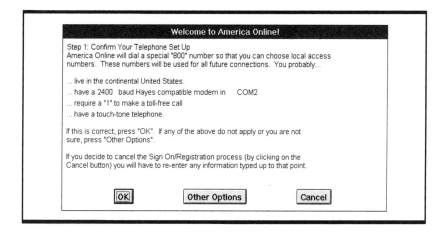

Figure 9.1
The first screen you'll get when you open America Online

If you have Call Waiting, you'll want to disable it for the duration of calls you make to AOL. Select Other Options and in the box shown in Figure 9.2, type ***70,** (1170, if you have a pulse phone). Include the comma. Click on OK.

Next, the software will call an 800 number so you can pick a local access phone number. You'll get to choose two access numbers, a first and a

Figure 9.2

Here's where you can disable Call Waiting for all the calls you make to America Online.

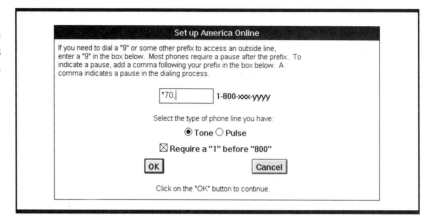

second choice. When you see the screen that looks like Figure 9.3, make sure you pick the best number for your location. Note the bps rating shown. You want to pick the nearest, fastest number.

The AOL software will then dial your first choice number and start the process of enrolling you.

Figure 9.3

Choosing a local access number

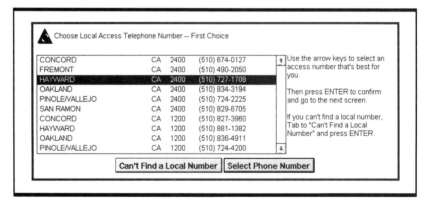

DOS Version

The DOS version of the software is not overly difficult to install, it just requires quite a few more steps and lots more participation on your part. The only real pitfall occurs if you have DOS 6.0 (or later) on your machine. If you do, see "Before You Install the DOS Software—Read This!"

You start by putting the software disk in your A: or B: drive. Change to that drive and type **Install**. Follow the instructions. If the software offers to make modifications to your setup for you, let it (unless you have a good reason not to). The software is pretty good at guessing your configuration, but you'll have to confirm some of the choices and supply some information yourself. For example, you'll have to specify what kind of printer you have and participate in setting up the video, mouse, and modem selections.

Before You Install the DOS Software— Read This!

America Online's DOS program is not the most forward-looking. The most recent version, 1.5a, works fine with earlier versions of DOS, but if you have DOS 6.0 or 6.2, you'll have to take a few extra steps to get the software to work.

First you have to add the following line to your CONFIG.SYS file:

```
DEVICE=C:\DOS\SETVER.EXE
```

Save the CONFIG.SYS file and reboot your computer. At the DOS prompt, type:

```
SETVER KERNEL.EXE 5.0
```

and press Enter. Disregard the alarming message you get and forge on. Next, type:

```
SETVER SETUP.EXE 5.0
```

and press Enter again. You'll get that same alarming message once more, but by now you should be used to it. Reboot your system.

Now put the AOL disk in the floppy-disk drive, change to that drive, and type **INSTALL**. Follow the instructions on the screen to install the program.

If, at the end of this procedure, your screen locks up and refuses to go forward, there's one additional step you'll have to take after rebooting your system. (You may even have to press the Reset button on your computer if the familiar Ctrl-Alt-Del doesn't work.)

Change to the AOL directory. Type:

```
EDIT AOL.BAT
```

This will open the DOS editor with the AOL.BAT file loaded. Edit the last line of this file so that it reads:

```
KERNEL /NOMEM
```

Save the file and exit DOS Edit. Now you should be able to type **AOL** and proceed with the enrollment process.

If this doesn't work, call the America Online Customer Support people at 1-800-787-7265.

And if all this strikes you as too tedious for words, call AOL and get the Windows version of the software, which will work on any machine that can get Windows to run.

 NOTE

In the DOS version of the software, you disable Call Waiting by clicking on Setup on the Welcome screen of America Online. There's an option on the Setup screen for disabling Call Waiting.

At the end of installation, you'll get a screen that looks a lot like Figure 9.1. In this screen, you'll get to change the settings that the software found, or accept them as-is. The software will dial an 800 number (Figure 9.4) and connect you with an America Online computer. This computer will provide you with a list of local phone numbers you can use for future calls. After you have selected your local numbers, the AOL software will dial your first choice and start you on the process of enrolling.

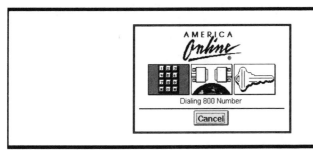

Enrolling

The next step is to answer all the same questions the on-line services usually ask: your name, address, and—that most important information—how you're going to pay for your fun.

You'll be asked to provide a password, which is usual in the world of on-line services. AOL, however, also asks you to provide a "screen name." This is a sort of nickname or "handle" by which you'll be known to others on the system. When you join a discussion or exchange e-mail, this is the name that will show up as yours.

You can use your first name, your last name, or a fanciful name of your own devising. If you use your first name or your first name and last initial, the software may suggest that you be "Bob5873" or "DebJ4909" so that if there're already folks with that name on the system, you get added to the end of the "Bob" queue or the "Deb" queue. On the other hand, a too cutesy name may become a hindrance later on. Consider your choice of this screen name carefully, because it cannot be changed or deleted later.

Getting Online

In the Windows version of AOL, you get online by double-clicking on the America Online icon. In the DOS version, you type **AOL** at the DOS prompt. In both cases, you'll be greeted with the Welcome screen. The Windows version is shown in Figure 9.5; the DOS version looks very much the same.

Figure 9.5

The Welcome screen

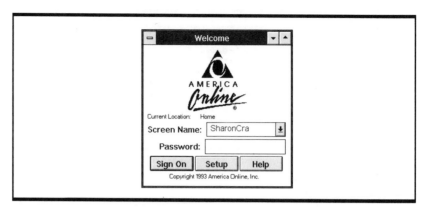

Your screen name will already be shown, but you have to type in your own password. Unlike CompuServe and Prodigy, there's no way to automate the password part of the process.

Fast Modem Speeds

Until recently, the fastest modem speed available to America Online was 2400bps. However, now 9600bps numbers are available in most parts of the country. If you have one of these nearby, you will find it a real time-saver. Even if the 9600bps node isn't the closest for you (in other words, it costs more to call the access number), it can still be helpful if you reserve it for those occasions when you want to download files.

 NOTE

Locations are alternative sign-on scenarios. For those times you take your computer on the road, for example, and access America Online from several different phone numbers.

Click on the Setup button on the Welcome screen and create a second Location. Give the Location a name that suits you and type in the 9600bps number you'll be using. Be sure to select 9600 from the Baud Rate drop-down list.

Use this Location when you are transferring files. The increase in transfer speed will more than compensate for any increase in telephone charges.

Like Prodigy (and conspicuously *un*like CompuServe), you can sign on to America Online at 9600bps without incurring any additional charges.

Having It Your Way

The America Online software is not especially configurable, but there are some variables to make your AOL experience more pleasant.

You can have up to five screen names associated with an account. For information on creating and deleting the secondary names, select Members Online Support under the Go To menu. Though you can't change the "master" screen name that you first signed on with, you can add and delete the other names when you want.

Select Preferences from the Members menu and you can set some general rules about downloading and fonts. The Windows version has Chat preferences here, as well as a place to change your password. When you first start using America Online, you should probably accept the default settings, until you know enough about the system to know what they mean.

After you've spent some time with the service and have some favorite spots you like to visit, you can modify the Go To menu to include those places. Select Go To ➤ Edit Go To Menu. Now you can remove stuff like Sign on a Friend (how often are you going to use that, after all?) and put in the places you go to regularly. You can list things under any name you like, as long as the keyword(s) are correct. Click on Save Changes and your menu will be modified.

Basic Principles of Navigation

When you first access AOL the first screen looks something like Figure 9.6. The larger buttons on the center window change from time to time. You can click on one of these if you want to see more.

An ideal place to start is the Discover AOL button. Click on that one and you'll get another screen. On this second screen click on the button called the Best of America Online. This will get you the list shown in Figure 9.7.

Figure 9.6

When you get online, this is
the screen you'll see first.

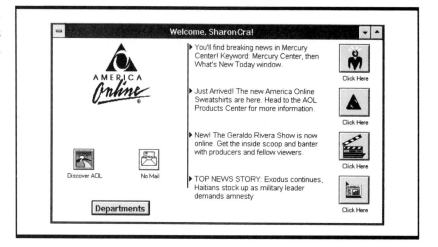

Figure 9.7

All the best stuff is on this list.

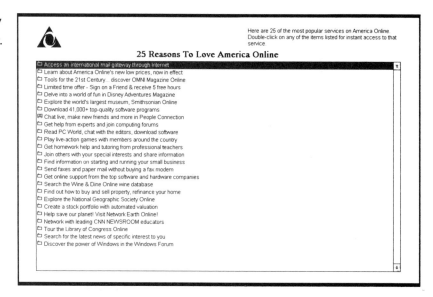

Click on any of the items in this list and you'll be whisked off to the area in question. For example, if you click on "Get help from experts and join computing forums," you'll be delivered to the Computing and Software window shown in Figure 9.8.

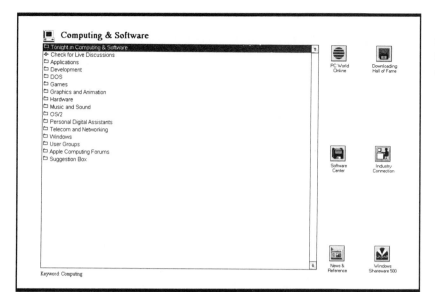

Want information on a particular manufacturer's hardware or software? Click on the Industry Connection button and get a list of all the manufacturers that are online, as shown in Figure 9.9. Select the connection you want.

For example, I have Symantec's Norton AntiVirus program on my computer and every few months I want to update the list of viruses the program knows about. So I select Symantec from the list and then Software Library, as seen in Figure 9.10.

In the library, I find the latest update (see Figure 9.11) and read the description (click on the Read Description button) to make sure it's what I want.

I press the Download Now button and tell the program where I want the new file to go (Figure 9.12).

 NOTE

As you go, make note of the keyword at the bottom of screens you want to return to. In the future, you can key in Ctrl-K (or select Keyword from the Go To menu) and go directly to the area you want by typing in the keyword.

Figure 9.9

A lot of the major manufacturers of software and hardware can be found in the Industry Connection.

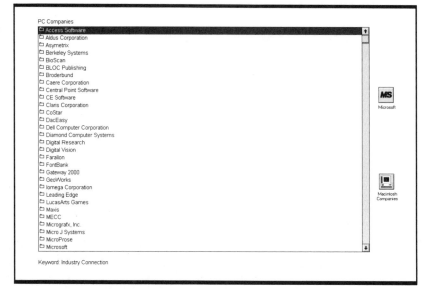

Figure 9.10

The list of subjects available in Symantec's on-line section

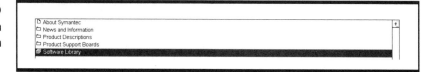

Figure 9.11

The list of files that can be downloaded from Symantec

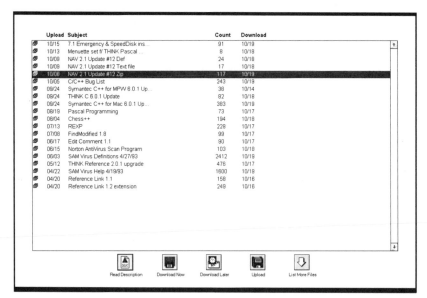

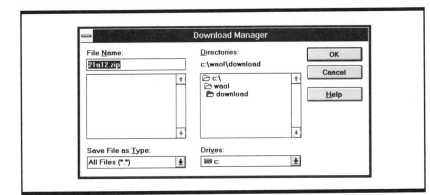

Figure 9.12
This is the default name and location. You can change the name of the file or where it goes.

The file is transferred to my computer (Figure 9.13) and when I leave America Online, it will be decompressed for me.

Among the best features in America Online are the enormous number of computer programs and other files available (at least 41,000 at any one time) and how easy it is to get them. Other on-line services have lots of downloadable files too, but none match the ease of access provided by AOL.

Another feature you might want to explore is the on-line Chat area. You can select "Chat live, make new friends and more in People Connection" from the screen shown in Figure 9.7.

Your first stop will be the lobby, as shown in Figure 9.14. You can hang around here and chat or just observe. You'll see how many people are in the lobby and their screen names at the top of the window. The conversation (from the time you dropped in) will scroll across the window.

 NOTE
Almost all the files available on AOL are compressed with the program PKZIP. One of the Preferences you can set has the program delete the original compressed file for you after it decompresses the contents. See "Inside Story" later in this chapter for more on PKZIP.

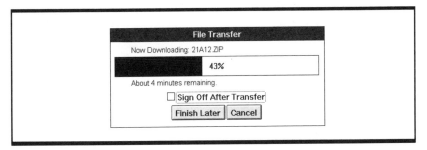

Figure 9.13
The file is transferred from Symantec's section at America Online to my computer.

Radio and TV on AOL

Some of the programs on National Public Radio, notably "Talk of the Nation," have an America Online connection. While "Talk of the Nation" is on the air (Monday–Friday, 2 PM ET), a parallel chat area is open on America Online. Use the keyword NPR. You can join in the discussion, find out how to order transcripts of other NPR programs, and download various files supplied by the NPR folks.

Some of the files I've downloaded are the "Talk of the Nation" summer reading list (with annotations) and Susan Stamberg's recipe for cranberry relish. It's a mixed bag, and very interesting.

For educational television, you can select the keyword KIDSNET for information on programs of quality. If that's too highbrow, you can also suggest program topics or order tickets for the Geraldo and Ricki Lake talk shows.

Believe me, it's accurately named *America* Online because everybody's represented here somehow!

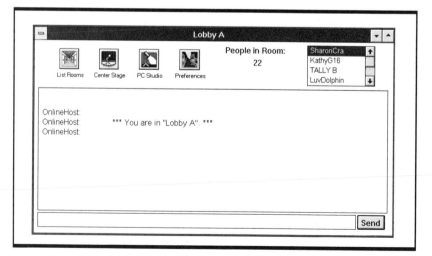

Figure 9.14

You're first deposited in an available lobby. As lobbies fill up, new ones are added, so you may find yourself in Lobby 2 or Lobby 3.

Click on the Rooms button to see what rooms are open and how many people are in each one. The maximum number in each room is 23. To enter a room, just select it. Figure 9.15 shows the Chat rooms on one particular day. Some of these rooms are open almost around the clock, others come and go.

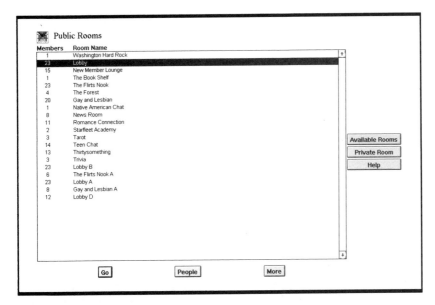

Figure 9.15
The public Chat rooms available on one particular day

Pick a room that interests you. It's considered polite to say hello when you enter, but you don't have to join in right away. Don't be afraid to join in when you have something to say. It's not considered rude. (People who want to have a private conversation, after all, will go into a private room.)

Also, don't be afraid to ask for help. People are remarkably friendly and welcoming online. It's a wonderful place for people who are even a little bit shy, because you don't have to talk if you don't want to and no one knows anything about you *except* what you say.

What's It Cost?

America Online is one of the most economical of the on-line services. The basic price is $9.95 a month, and that includes five hours of on-line time. After five hours, the price is $3.50 per hour. Of course, it's possible for an on-line junkie to run up a humongous bill even so, but most people will find the costs to be reasonable.

All the services are billed at the same rate, except for the following:

Quantum Space	A play-by-mail game. For information see the text under the keyword QSPACE.
Fax/Paper Mail	Sending a fax costs $2 per address (a lot cheaper than the corner copy store). Paper mail costs $2.50 per address. For information see the keyword FAX.
Store charges	Obviously if you order a product online, that will cost extra and will be included on your monthly bill.
Members' On-line Support	Time spent here is not charged against your account.

You can pay for your account using MasterCard, Visa, American Express, or Discover; or you can have the amount deducted from your checking account every month.

Saving Money on America Online

The most important way to save money on AOL is to minimize the amount of time you spend online. This is true of all the on-line services, but America Online makes it more difficult than some of the others.

Two of the best things about America Online are also real time-eaters. First there are the on-line chats. You can use up an hour or two without the slightest bit of effort. The CompuServe strategy of signing on at 300bps for live sessions doesn't work here, because the same rate is charged regardless of the modem speed chosen. If you're going to be chatting in the conference rooms, sign on at the closest, cheapest possible access phone number. The baud rate doesn't matter much because no one writes messages faster than 300bps anyway.

Generally try to stay alert and don't zone out. You can check the amount of time you've been gabbing by clicking on the alarm clock button on the button bar.

Another good thing about America Online is all the downloadable files and graphics. But if you're fetching these files using a 2400bps modem, it can take quite a long time. Here's where a 9600bps node can be especially helpful. If you can sign on at 9600bps the file transfer will be about four times faster.

You can also save money by composing your mail offline then signing on and sending it.

Use the Logging feature in the File menu to keep a record of your online session so you can read things offline when you're not paying for the time. Select Logging from the file menu and get the dialog box shown in Figure 9.16.

Select Open and give a name to the log. Click on OK. After you sign off America Online, you can select Open from the file menu and select the log and read everything at your leisure.

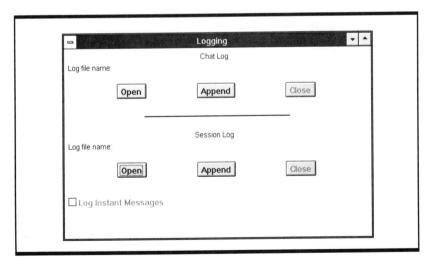

Figure 9.16
You can make a chat log or a log of the whole session.

Inside Story

If you have a problem, you can get help either online or by calling 1-800-787-7265. The phone support is considerably better. The Customer Support people you reach by phone are both knowledgeable and patient. Who could ask for more than that?

The on-line people may be smart, too, but it's hard to tell. Generally when you post a message to the customer support people online, you get a canned response. The response may deal with the question you asked or it may not. No one seems to actually *read* the question. So unless you can find the answer in the Member Support section, waste no time and go directly to the phone people.

Compressed Files

Almost all the files you'll get from America Online will be compressed with the world's most popular shareware program, PKZIP. If you want to upload a file to America Online (send it from your computer to theirs), you'll also be asked to compress the program with PKZIP. PKZIP squishes files down so they can be transmitted much faster. When you receive a file on AOL that has been compressed by PKZIP, the America Online software will automatically unzip it for you and restore it to its normal size.

 **NOTE**
There's more on using PKZIP and PKUNZIP in Chapter 16.

PKZIP itself can be downloaded from AOL. If you don't have PKZIP, get it and register it. You can find it by using the keywords File Search, then search for PKZIP. The one you want is called PKZ110.EXE.

PKZ110.EXE is what's called a self-extracting archive (the other kind of compressed file you'll find on America Online). You download it, but in this case AOL's automatic decompression doesn't kick in. You have to go to the DOS prompt in the directory where you deposited PKZ110.EXE. Then type **PKZ110** and out will pop all the programs and files inside. You may want to also download the latest version of PKZIP 2.x. This is an up-and-coming compression program, but because it works completely differently from PKZIP 1.x, you probably will need both—at least for a while.

Parents' Rights

Since you can have multiple screen names, it stands to reason that more than one household member can sign on to America Online. If you have included one or more rugrats on your membership, you can use the Parental Control feature to restrict access. Use the select keyword from the Go To menu and type **Parental Control** to get more information.

A Final Note

America Online is fairly easy to use even if it is a little confusing at first. It doesn't cost an arm and a leg, especially if you have a 9600bps access number close at hand. You'll have to spend some time exploring and making notes to yourself about the features that interest you. After you know what your favorite spots *are*, you can modify the Go To menu to automate your way.

AOL has a strong bias in favor of events that take place live. Famous people drop in for conferences and chats both announced and impromptu.

America Online has the undeniable asset of having a one-price-for-almost-everything policy. All you have to worry about is the total amount of time you're spending chatting with friends or downloading files.

Ten

The Internet

• •

Y ou've probably heard something about the "information superhighway." Sure you have, it's been in all the papers. It all sounds very Flash Gordon and Star Trekkie. But the fact is, the information superhighway is being built on a foundation that exists today. That foundation is called the Internet, and you can go there now—not ten years from now.

Unlike all the on-line services discussed in previous chapters, the Internet is not a commercial enterprise. It is, in fact, a network of many other networks that grew out of a 1960s project of the Department of Defense called the Advanced Research Projects Agency (ARPA). In fact, the earliest name for what is now the Internet was the ARPAnet. Other government and research institutions joined in over the years. This network of networks enabled scientists and scholars to communicate directly, if not always instantly.

In the late 1980s, the National Science Foundation funded an upgrade that included high-speed lines to link a dozen or so super-computer sites around the country. At the same time, a number of regional networks were linked to the super-computer centers. Some of these regional networks began selling accounts to ordinary businesses and individuals, and the Internet (also called the "Net") came into being.

Today, the Net is so large and complex that no one knows exactly how many computers are on it or how many people are actually using it. There are millions of people using tens of thousands of networks in at least 100 countries—and you can communicate with any of them!

Use of the Internet requires a willingness to learn and explore. The Internet has generated a new vocabulary of terms that can look very peculiar until you learn them. Like all such learning processes, this one requires patience and persistence. Your patience at the beginning will pay off handsomely in the end, because the wealth of information and contacts available through the Internet is unmatched anywhere.

 NOTE

Most of the computers supplying services on the Internet are running the UNIX operating system. That's why the commands look so peculiar. But you don't have to know UNIX (thank heavens!) to use the Internet, and you'll only have to learn a half-dozen or so commands to get by.

What'll I Find There?

 NOTE

You'll probably not want to launch yourself on the Internet until you've had a chance to explore an on-line service and/or a few local bulletin boards. Going straight to the Internet is like learning to drive on an interstate highway at rush hour—exciting, but perhaps not the best place to start.

One of the most popular things on the Internet is NetNews, which amounts to some 3–4 thousand discussion groups. Or you can send private e-mail to any of the millions of folks who use Internet. Or you can directly log on to computers funded by NASA, or the main library in Munich, or the archives of Yeshiva University.

NetNews

These groups are roughly analogous to the forums on CompuServe, except that they are much larger and there are many more of them. The news groups that'll be available to you once you get to the Internet will depend on the news server you have access to, and that depends on where you sign on and with what service. Suffice it to say, there will be many. The news groups will be organized under several broad headings.

Each of the following groups has hundreds of subcategories:

comp	Computer science and related topics
news	News about NetNews itself and its administration, including groups with important information for new users
talk	Forums for long, unresolved debate on controversial topics—if you want to argue about religion or gun control or other such stuff, this is the place
rec	Recreational topics, including hobbies and the arts
sci	Scientific topics, usually related to research in or application of the established sciences
soc	Social issues, including politics
alt	Some of the weirdest stuff (there are rules for creating new groups under other headings, but anyone can create an alt news group.)
misc	Groups addressing anything that incorporates themes from other groups, such as job offerings and resume postings

In addition to these groups, the server may collect news from other sources as well as create groups that exist just locally.

News groups are organized with the broadest grouping appearing first in the name, followed by the subgroupings, so:

    rec.dance.mod

is a discussion in the recreation group, about dance, and more specifically about modern dance. In the same grouping, you may find:

    rec.dance.ballet

which is, of course, a discussion group for balletomanes.

E-Mail

Access to the Internet also gives you access to one of the fastest and most convenient mail systems ever invented. You can send e-mail to people all over the world or just down the block. You can even include a file with your message and send it to a hundred people as easily as to one.

Research

Though the Internet was originally designed for high-end scientific and military research, there's a lot out there for those of us more securely planted at the low end. You can find amazing quantities of software, search databases of all kinds, and retrieve documents from here to Honduras.

Getting to the Internet

The Internet is not a commercial enterprise, but getting to the Internet usually involves some money changing hands. Getting access is actually trickier than getting around once you get there.

If you belong to one of the big on-line services, such as CompuServe or America Online, you'll see that they offer "gateways" to the Internet. However, that gateway is only for e-mail. This is not to be scorned, of course, but it's far from a full picture. It's like seeing Disneyland through a knothole in the fence.

What you need is an Internet *account*. If you're a student or otherwise affiliated with a university, you may be able to get a free account through that institution.

 NOTE

Even if you get one through school or work, the account may have limits placed on it. For example, your company may actually expect you to use the account only for work-related subjects! Or the account may not get a full feed of NetNews and you'll miss out on groups you'd like to see.

You may be able to get an account through your job. Many companies, not just those in the computer industry, have Internet connections and you may be able to get the best kind of account—a free one—that way. Check with the network administrator or the MIS department.

For the rest of us, the alternative is a commercial service. There are a lot of them; the best one for you is probably going to be in your area. This is because the cost of using the service is only part of the picture. You also have to consider the cost of the phone connection. Even if the service charges only $10 a month, it's no bargain if you have to call long distance and pay the phone company $10 an hour (or more) for the time you're online.

Bear in mind that the commercial services are not all created equal. Some offer Internet access in a way that requires either a lot of previous communications knowledge or a very high tolerance for frustration. The degree of on-line help ranges from the extensive to the virtually nonexistent. All have their own "culture" and that, too, ranges all over the map.

It's beyond the scope of this book to list all the commercial services that provide wide access (in other words, the full range of Internet services). We can, however, discuss places to start.

Lists of Commercial Accounts

If you have a friend or colleague with Internet access, ask this charming person to print out a copy of PDIAL for you. This, as well as several other lists of public access systems, can be found in the NewsNet postings. PDIAL is the most extensive of these lists, showing dozens of systems that offer full Internet access. If you already have a CompuServe account, you can download a recent version of PDIAL from the libraries of the Electronic Frontier Foundation (EFF) forum. The EFF's libraries are full of great information about the Internet.

Or you can look in local computer publications in your area. They're likely to list bulletin boards that have Internet access. One source is the hefty publication, *Computer Shopper*. Every month they list hundreds of bulletin boards by telephone area code (one half of the U.S. one month, the other half the next month). Many of the boards listed include Internet features.

In Table 10.1, you'll find a list of public access services for the Internet. This list is not exhaustive—that would be a much longer list that would be out of date as soon as it was committed to paper. However, the services in the list are meant to be geographically representative, generally not require prior membership in a special group, and offer full Internet access.

Delphi

Delphi is just one of the many services that offer Internet access. I include it here because it's one of the easiest places to get started. You can call them from anywhere in the U.S. and get started without being an on-line genius.

Table 10.1

How to connect to the Internet

Company	Area Covered	Voice Phone Number
Alternet	U.S. and international	800-488-6383
Anomaly	Rhode Island	401-273-4669
ANS	U.S. and international	313-663-7610
BARRNet	Northern and central California	415-723-7520
CERFNet	Western U.S. and international	800-876-2373
CICNet	Midwestern U.S.	313-998-6102
Communications Accessible Montreal	Quebec	514-923-2102
ConnectCOM Australia	Australia	+61 3 5282239
COSupernet	Colorado	303-273-3471
CONCERT	North Carolina	919-248-1404
CSUnet	California	310-985-9661
DELPHI	U.S.	800-544-4005
Halcyon	Washington	206-955-1050
Interaccess	Chicago, IL	708-671-0111
INet	Indiana	812-855-4240
JVNCNet	U.S. and international	800-358-4437
Los Nettos	Los Angeles, CA	310-822-1511
Metronet	Dallas, TX	214-401-2800
MichNet	Michigan	313-764-9430
MIDNet	Midwestern U.S.	402-472-5032
MindVOX	New York, NY	212-988-5987
NEARNet	Northeastern U.S.	617-873-8730
Netcom	California	408-554-8649
NetIllinois	Illinois	309-677-3100
NevadaNet	Nevada	702-784-6133
NYSERNet	New York	315-453-2912

Company	Area Covered	Voice Phone Number	Table 10.1
OARNet	Ohio	614-292-8100	How to connect to the Internet
PACCOM	Hawaii	808-946-3499	
Public Access Unix (PANIX)	New York, NY	212-877-4854	
PREPNet	Pennsylvania	412-268-7870	
Sesquinet	Texas	713-527-4988	
Sugar Land Unix	Houston, TX	713-438-4964	
SURANet	Southeastern U.S.	301-982-4600	
UK PC User Group	London	+44 (0)81 863 6646	
VERNet	Virginia	804-924-0616	
The Well	U.S.	415-332-4335	
WiscNet	Wisconsin	608-262-8874	
The World	Boston, MA	617-739-0202	
WVNet	West Virginia	304-293-5192	

You start by opening your general-purpose communications program and telling it to dial 1-800-365-4636. (The number for voice calls is 800-544-4005.)

When you get an answer, press the Enter key once or twice until you see:

User name:

Type **JOINDELPHI**. At Password, enter **INTERNETSIG** and you'll get a screen like that shown in Figure 10.1.

If you continue and register, you'll get a local phone number for future calls. When you call that number you'll be hooked into a phone network—either Sprintnet or Tymnet. (Both Sprintnet and Tymnet are widely used by Prodigy and America Online as well.) This phone network will then connect you to DELPHI. The Sprintnet or Tymnet connection for DELPHI is free nights and weekends, but will cost you $9 per hour during weekday business hours (7AM to 6PM—your local time). The charge will be included on the credit card account you supply to DELPHI when you register.

 NOTE

If you're using ProComm Plus, you won't have to do anything except dial the number. ProComm will connect at the fastest possible speed using all the right connections. With other programs you may have to specify VT-100 terminal emulation and no parity, 8 data bits, and 1 stop bit. Call the voice number if you have a problem connecting.

Figure 10.1

The opening screen for DELPHI

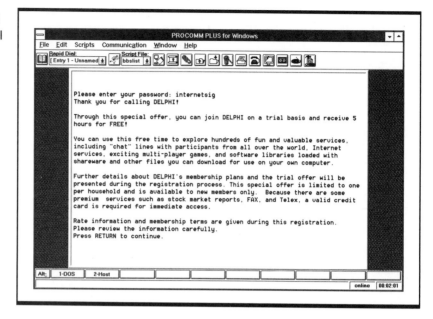

DELPHI is a lot more than just access to the Internet, as you can see from Figure 10.2.

Figure 10.2

DELPHI is a full-featured on-line service, in addition to offering Internet access.

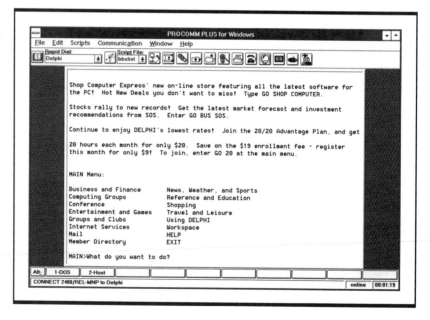

To get to the Internet services, you'll need to register. Type **GO IN-TERNET** at any prompt. This will take you to the main menu for the Internet SIG (Special Interest Group), where you can register. The main menu is shown in Figure 10.3.

 NOTE

Access to the Internet will cost you another $3 per month over DELPHI's usual prices.

Figure 10.3
The Internet SIG's main menu

After you've registered, look around. One of the best things about DELPHI as an Internet connection is the quantity and quality of information helping you to use all the Internet features.

For example, before you're on the Internet for very long, you'll hear about a program called *Gopher*. It's designed to be used by novices and helps you retrieve information from machines on the Internet. In fact, it's one of the best tools for gathering information, because it has a standard interface. In other words, it looks the same to you regardless of where you're gathering the information from.

 NOTE

Why Gopher? The most common answer is because it was developed by programmers at the University of Minnesota, whose mascot is the Golden Gopher. It's also meant to be a "go-fer" as on one who "goes for" things. Another, equally valid, answer is "Why not?" After all, Internet is full of other programs with names like **Finger**, **Archie**, and **Veronica**.

To get information on Gopher, type **Gopher** when you're at the main menu. You'll get a screen like that shown in Figure 10.4.

Figure 10.4

A whole lot about Gopher

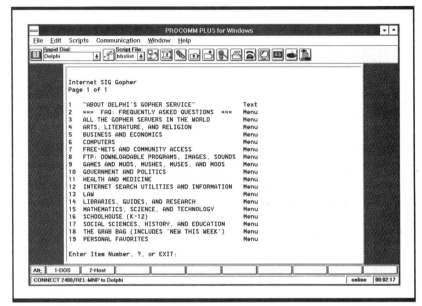

Read the first two items on the list and you'll be ready to start. As you can see just from the variety of topics shown, it's a very big Internet world out there.

For direct assistance, you can also post a message in the Forum (also on the Internet main menu) or by participating in one of the regular conferences.

Figure 10.5 shows the list of frequently asked questions about Gopher. You can see that there're a lot of answers available.

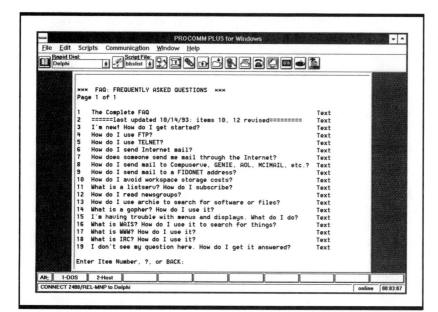

Figure 10.5
DELPHI's "most frequently asked question" screen for Gopher

Other Service Providers

One of the limitations of using DELPHI (or any other service using the Sprintnet or Tymnet networks) is that you get access only at 2400bps or slower. To get faster access, either you can find a provider in your area code that offers 9600bps or you can look for a service that uses a CompuServe Packet Network (CPN) node. For a few dollars an hour (depending on distance and time), you can use Internet service providers such as The Well (Whole Earth 'Lectronic Link) in Sausalito, California, or The World in Boston, Massachusetts.

Both of these services are cheap enough to be reasonable even after adding the $4-$5 per hour that using a CPN costs.

For The Well, use your communications software to dial 415-332-6106 and sign on as "newuser." You'll be walked through the whole process of signing up. This is another case where they ask you to pick a handle and you're stuck with it forever, so you'd better like it.

The Well has a really archaic interface that makes absolutely nothing easy for you, and their system for getting information from the tech support folks online stinks. However, subscribers to The Well are much

NOTE
To get a local number for the CompuServe Packet Network, call 1-800-848-8980. This is a voice call. You don't need to belong to CompuServe to use a CPN number.

NOTE
The Well was recently sold and the new owners have promised big improvements.

more fanatically attached to their service than are the subscribers to other services. If you're interested in the lastest news from the cyber-space frontier, The Well is the place to check out. If you want other information, the voice number is 415-332-4335.

For the modestly-named The World, call 617-739-9753 and sign on as "new." Their voice number is 617-739-0202. Don't get excited when they answer the phone as "Software Tool and Die," that's the name of the company that runs the service. The World is probably a better choice if you live in the eastern half of the United States.

NOTE

For some services, you'll be given an 800 number for registration but the actual "use" number will be one that you have to pay for.

A number of services have 800 numbers you can use for access, but they're not exactly cheap. The least expensive I could find was the Community News Service in Colorado. They charge $8 per hour for 800 phone service from anywhere in the continental U.S. (If you live in the 303 or 719 area code it's considerably cheaper.) Have the modem dial them at 719-520-1700 and use the ID "new."

Generally what you want to do is get connected with a service that feels reasonably comfortable and friendly. Get acquainted with the Internet (or at least start the process) for a few months. At some point, use your new Internet skills to get PDIAL or another list of Internet providers. From that list, you can check out service providers close to home. You may well find one that has all the features you want and is only a local call away.

What a Service Should Provide

Because the commercial services are so varied, you may have to look around for a while before finding one you like (and one that is afford-able). Here are some of the features the more complete services offer.

File Transfer Protocol

File Transfer Protocol, generally known as FTP, is a service that enables you to transfer files to and from other computers on the Internet. Without FTP, a service is limited to e-mail and NetNews. On most services, when you use FTP a copy of every file you request is transferred to your personal workspace. From there you can download it to your own computer.

For example, on DELPHI you just type **FTP** at the Internet menu. You'll need the Internet address of the computer from which you want to retrieve files. It's usually helpful also to know the filenames and directories where they are located. You can find addresses of some popular FTP sites in the Internet area on DELPHI.

Telnet

Telnet is used to actually log in to other computers on the Internet. The majority of host computers on the Internet require you to have an account before you log in, but some maintain guest accounts. For example, if you were logging in to the World or DELPHI from some location on the Internet, you'd need to be a registered user, just as you'd need to be when logging in from your own computer.

If signing on to remote computers is something you'll want to do, make sure you get an account with a service that offers Telnet. The Well lets you use Telnet, but they don't make it easy. DELPHI puts it right on the main Internet menu.

Gopher

As mentioned above, Gopher is a look-up tool that lets you "tunnel" around the Internet. It lets you browse through the resources available, read text files, and retrieve files of all kinds.

If the pre-Gopher Internet was like an uncatalogued library, then the Internet with Gopher is like libraries catalogued by none-too-skilled librarians who didn't consult with each other. For example, there's no standard filing system, so material covering the same subject may be under different category headings on different Gopher servers.

However, Gopher has a menu system that's not too difficult to understand. And Gopher is also easier to use than to describe, as you'll discover when you try it out.

Archie and Veronica

Archie is a powerful utility that will search for specific files in FTP archives across the Internet. If you know the name of a file, Archie will search the list it keeps and tell you where the file is located. You can then use FTP to retrieve it.

Veronica is a program that works a lot like Archie, except that it searches Gopherspace—repositories of Gopher files. You give Veronica a keyword and it searches the areas it knows for that keyword.

WAIS: Wide Area Information System

WAIS (pronounced "ways") allows you to search more than 300 information sources by keyword. It's easy to start but it's not so easy to use. It's best at searches for academic material. Future versions of WAIS may make it easier to use.

Once you get familiar with some of the other tools, you may want to try WAIS. If you do, you'll need assistance to formulate your search criteria, so look for a service that has these help files available.

Finger and Whois

Finger and Whois are utilities (and in the case of Whois, both a directory *and* a utility) for locating other Internet users. There are now millions of users on the Net and, unfortunately, there's no single directory of users that you can search to find a particular person. But if you have a person's name and Internet address, you may be able to find them.

Better utilities are being developed to help find individuals on the Internet. That's an idea whose time is overdue.

World-Wide Web

The World-Wide Web (WWW) is one of the most exciting developments on the Internet today. It's a "hypertext" service that connects widely scattered documents with "links" to other documents. You can jump to any linked document, which in turn may be linked to other documents. That way you can pursue a line of inquiry as far as you want.

Currently, the amount of information available through WWW is not vast, but it is growing. WWW offers a tantalizing glimpse of what the Internet may be like in the future.

Shells

Most of the public access accounts for Internet are on computers running UNIX. UNIX offers different *shells*, or ways to communicate with the operating system. If you're a UNIX user, you'll want to pick a service that uses the shell you're familiar with. If you don't know much about UNIX, just accept the default if you're offered a choice.

Help

For the beginner, the most important attribute a commercial service can offer is help. Only a few of the Internet programs and utilities even remotely resemble anything you've seen in the world of DOS or Windows. None require a genius to navigate, but they *are* new and they will require time to learn.

Lots of easily available lists of FAQs (Frequently Asked Questions) are an asset. An on-line forum or discussion area is even better. There you can post a question or ask about a problem, and have it answered quickly. If you don't understand the answer, you can ask for clarification.

This is one of the reasons I like DELPHI. It excels in the area of help and on-line support. There may be some who do almost as well and others are scrambling to catch up, but for the present, DELPHI is still the service to beat.

Basic Principles of Navigation

The Internet is divided into logical collections of machines known as *domains*. Unlike zip codes or area codes that are always geographic, the networks that make up the Internet are divided into conceptual groups, such as educational, government, military, and commercial enterprises. These domains are known loosely as top-level domains. The major domestic domains are:

com	Commercial organizations
edu	Educational institutions like universities
gov	Nonmilitary government agencies
mil	Military institutions
org	Other organizations
net	Network providers

The format for e-mail addresses demonstrates the concept of domains. The basic format is *userid@hostname*. For example, my account at America Online has the Internet e-mail address:

sharoncra@aol.com

This says that there is a specific user ID called *sharoncra* on the computer system called *aol* in the *com*merical domain. This addressing system would be simplicity itself if all the computers in the world had unique names. But many organizations are divided into subdomains. Here's another, fictitious, example. To reach a user with the user ID *melnick* who uses a computer called *einstein* in the *phys*ics department at the University of California at *Berkeley*, the address might be:

melnick@einstein.phys.berkeley.edu

When you use a name like this, the network computer needs to turn it into an address, starting from the right. If your local service doesn't know the address (it might know, especially if the address is local), your network computer contacts a root server that has all the addresses for servers in the *edu* domain. Looking at all the *edu* addresses, it finds the address for *berkeley*. The network computer then calls the *berkeley* computer and asks for the address of the server for *phys*. Then the *phys* server is quizzed for the address of *einstein*. When *einstein* is located,

 NOTE

Unfortunately, most addresses are not this clear. They'll look like **llgaus@eco.fgtf.hr.net** or something equally cryptic. Over time, you'll learn to recognize the ones you use a lot. Besides, most software lets you put the address of someone sending you e-mail into your address book, so you won't have to keep track of it yourself.

the mail is deposited in the mailbox for *melnick*. All this happens re-markably quickly and, in many cases, virtually instantaneously.

In all cases, the search starts from the largest category and proceeds to the smallest. Here's another example:

jkirk@enterprise.nasa.gov

In this case, the search starts with all the computers in the *gov* domain. It proceeds to the subdomain called *nasa* and then proceeds to the computer called *enterprise*.

This same principal is in effect when you want to specify a particular computer for a search. Reading from the right side of the address and proceeding to the left, the address proceeds from the larger domain to increasingly small ones until it reaches one particular and unique computer.

In the example above, the computer name *enterprise* can apply only to one computer. In order for the government to have another computer named *enterprise*, it would have to be in another subdomain (for example, *enterprise.nasa.gov* and *enterprise.subs4.dod.gov* are different computers, each with its own unique name).

Outside the United States, the top-level domain used in an Internet address is usually a two-letter country code. Some are easy to decipher, like UK for the United Kingdom and IT for Italy. But you could also get e-mail from VU (Vanuatu) or KK (Kazakhstan).

A Final Note

The Internet is so large and the methods of accessing it so different, it's impossible to compare it to anything else, except to say that it's the world's largest electronic library.

Unlike any other library, it's not organized under any one system, so finding your way around is not so methodical as in a real library. It will take some time, effort, and money to become comfortable with even a part of the Internet. Nevertheless, it's neither necessary nor desirable to become an expert on every facet of the Internet. (Not if you want to have a family and a job, too.) It's too big and exploring can be too all-consuming.

You may also have to shop around to find a commercial access point that suits you; most of them are not advertised in the press (at least not yet).

There are few places as intriguing and exciting as the Internet in the world of telecommunications. It's the one place where ordinary people can see the future before it's arrived.

Eleven

Bulletin Boards

• •

In the early days of modem communications, bulletin boards were the most popular places for people to hang out—to get new software, exchange ideas and information, and just generally schmooze. With the rise of the big commercial systems, like CompuServe and Prodigy, bulletin boards have fallen from prominence. But they still remain a valuable resource for certain types of information, and even more important, for a sense of community that's lacking both on the big systems and in many peoples' lives.

What is a Bulletin Board?

A bulletin board (also called a BBS) is a small on-line service usually run by one or two people. It can also be run by a special interest group or a company. For example, the company that made your modem probably has a bulletin board. In fact, it may well have been the first place you called after installing your modem.

Many manufacturers also run bulletin boards. You may have to call long distance to reach them, but these BBSs can provide upgrades, bug fixes, new printer drivers, and other help that you need. Assuming that you have a relatively fast modem (9600bps or better), you can get what you need pretty quickly.

The typical bulletin board is privately run and consists of one or more PCs (or Macintoshes) with several modems and phone lines. The operators will be running special bulletin-board software that lets them set up message sections, conferences, software libraries, and so forth.

Some bulletin boards are highly specialized. In the state of Pennsylvania alone, there are bulletin boards that specialize in science fiction, legal issues, music, engineering, AutoCAD, matchmaking, dinosaurs, the occult, scuba diving, and computer technical support. You can find bulletin boards that revolve around collectibles, antique cars, the ever-present "adult graphics" (read "porn" ranging from soft to medium-hard), Internet news feeds, commercial real estate, and on and on.

Most BBSs, however, offer a range of services. The most common include messaging, conferences, shareware and graphics libraries, games, and news feeds of one type or another.

Pluses

The plus of bulletin boards is that they're cheaper than any commercial service. Even the bulletin boards that are run for a profit are much less expensive to use than CompuServe or Prodigy would be for the same amount of time. Also, when you join a bulletin board, you can often form on-line friendships with many people.

Minuses

Because BBSs are run by individuals using individual PCs, they can experience more down time than a commercial service. The system may crash, taking your messages (or even the fact that you're a member) with it, and may remain offline for days while the owner fixes the system.

The local friendliness inherent in a bulletin board can also limit its usefulness for certain purposes. If you're a hydrologist looking to exchange tips with other hydrologists, you're better off on a national service. It's possible that there's a bulletin board just for hydrologists somewhere—but it probably won't be a local call.

How to Find Bulletin Boards

Bulletin boards are listed in almost every regional computer publication—such as *MicroTimes*, a free monthly distributed in the Northern California area. These local publications have the most complete and extensive listings. There are probably a couple thousand BBSs scattered across the country. Most are located in areas where the population is concentrated—the urban and suburban belts—but there are plenty even in the most thinly populated areas. You should start looking locally before you get attached to a BBS in a different area code, because even a free BBS can become expensive when you start incurring long-distance charges.

If you don't know of a regional computer publication in your area, hie to the nearest large news stand and buy a copy of the very hefty publication, *Computer Shopper*. This publication lists so many bulletin boards, it has to divide them up and print only Alabama through Michigan one month, followed by Minnesota through Wyoming the next. (The Minnesota-through-Wyoming issue also includes listings for a number of BBSs in Canada and a few other countries).

The listings are by state and by area code within the state. Each listing has quite a bit of information, if you know how to translate it. For example, here's one in Pennsylvania with accompanying translation:

York 840-1444	The name of the town the BBS is located in and the phone number you call to reach it.
Cyberia—The Final Stop in Cyberspace	The name of the BBS. Sometimes it gives you a hint of the place and sometimes it doesn't.
Sysop Adam & Sara Viener	The names of the sysops. *Sysop* is short for System Operator—in this case it's a couple. The sysop, who is the head honcho on the BBS, sets all the rules and has the final say on everything.
9 lines—486	The number of phone lines for people to call up on and the computer being used; in this case a PC with a 80486 processor.
1200MB	The amount of disk storage. In this case, it's enough to demonstrate that the BBS probably has quite a few files available and room for a number of different features.
TBBS 2.2M with U.S. Robotics	The software they're running and the modems they use. This is not of particular interest unless you're a fan of various bulletin board software programs and know which ones do what. It matters very little to the person calling in to use the BBS.
57600bps	The maximum access speed. This is important if you're looking to download files and want to do it as quickly as possible.
Established 6/93	The year the BBS was established. A relatively new BBS, this one's probably anxious to recruit new users. That makes this a good place to look for free connect time.

No fee   Don't take this entry too seriously. It's
                true that some BBSs are actually free, but
                most cost something. In this case,
                Cyberia will let you online for 25
                minutes per day indefinitely—for no fee.
                However, access to some features
                requires membership, which is $7 per
                month for two hours per day of usage.

This information is followed by a list of features that the BBS offers,
such as games, graphics files, or special interest discussion groups.

Getting Online

To call a BBS, you'll need a communications program such as Pro-
Comm or Microlink or Crosstalk. In general, you should use the default settings and let the software make the connection for you.

When I first called Cyberia (the BBS described above), I got a screen
that looked like Figure 11.1. This was not what I expected.

```
        \[[\
       ^[  []
        \^[ [[[\
        \[[^[[[[[[\
\[[[[[[[[[[[[[[[[[[ [[[ [[[ [[[[[[\ [[[[[[ [[[[[\ [[[ \[[[[[\
^[[ [[[[^[          [[[\[[[ [[[\[[_ [[[\\  [[[\[[[ [[[ [[[\[[[
_[[[]  ^[        ^[[[ _[[[_ [[[_[[[ [[[__   [[[_[[\ [[[ [[[_[[[
    _[[^[   \       [[[  [[[[[[[_ [[[[[[[ [[[ [[[ [[[ [[[
    -,^[                        The Final Stop In Cyberspace
    ^[ []                       717-840-1444
ZDDDDDDDDDD_[[_DDDDDDDDDDDDDDDDDDDDDDDDDDDDDDDDDDDDDDDDDDDDDDDD?
3 ZDDDDDDDDDD?    ZDDDDDDDDD?  ZDDDDDDDDDDDDDDDDDDDDDDDDDDDDDDDDDDDDDD? 3
3 3 York, PA 3  3 Welcome! 3  3 USRobotics 16.8 Dual Standards On All Lines 3 3
3 @DDDDDDDDDDY  @DDDDDDDDDDY  @DDDDDDDDDDDDDDDDDDDDDDDDDDDDDDDDDDDDDDY 3
3 ZDDDDDDDDDDDDDDDDDDDDDDDDDDDDDDDDDDDDDDDDDDDDDDDDDDDDDDDDDDDDDDD? 3
3 3                      Welcome to Cyberia!                      3 3
3 3                                                              3 3
3 3              Nightowl 10 CD Now Available Online!            3 3
3 @DDDDDDDDDDDDDDDDDDDDDDDDDDDDDDDDDDDDDDDDDDDDDDDDDDDDDDDDDDDDDDDY 3
@DDDDDDDDDDDDDDDDDDDDDDDDDDDDDDDDDDDDDDDDDDDDDDDDDDDDDDDDDDDDDDDDDDY
-Press Any Key-
```

Figure 11.1
If you get a screen that looks
like this, you may have the
wrong terminal setting.

So I hung up, changed the terminal setting from VT100 (which knows nothing about graphics) to ANSI BBS (which does) and got the screen shown in Figure 11.2. This was more like it.

Figure 11.2

The new and improved screen, after I changed the terminal setting

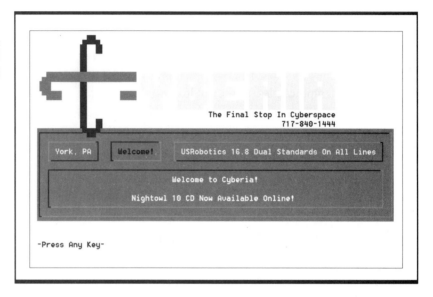

Many BBSs will ask you when you first log on if you want a graphics interface. The graphics interface is much nicer looking, but will slow things down a bit. The majority of smaller bulletin boards use text only, but you can still use ANSI BBS as your terminal setting. It'll work fine.

Registration is usually easy. You'll be asked for your name, address, and phone number, and that all-important credit card information (for those BBSs that charge for their services). Most of the time, that will give you instant access to whatever the BBS offers. A few of the more prudent actually call you back to verify that you're who you say you are.

Every bulletin board is different. This is part of their charm and, of course, part of the problem, too. You'll have to call up each one you're interested in and check it out. Newer bulletin board services often offer free connect time so you can explore without committing yourself. If a service looks interesting, join for a month. You can always cancel your registration if you find that you're either not using it or it doesn't meet your needs.

Basic Principles of Navigation

As a rule, bulletin boards do their best to make it easy to get around. The next few figures show a typical bulletin board. In fact, I picked it out of *Computer Shopper's* listings solely because it was the closest one to home.

When I called the number the first time, I got the screen shown in Figure 11.3.

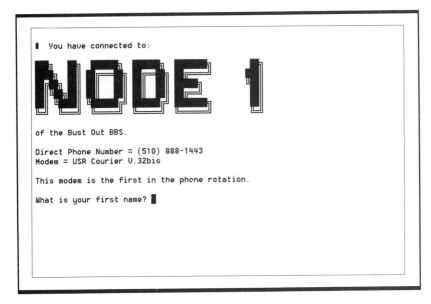

Figure 11.3
A sign-on screen for a fairly typical bulletin board

After I supplied my name and address and phone number, I got the screens shown in Figures 11.4 and 11.5.

This bulletin board provides 20 minutes of free time for the new user to browse around (though I found this out only by accident when I was poking around), and if you're interested enough, a free one-week trial membership.

Figure 11.4

Information about the bulletin board's offerings, as well as what you can get as a new user

```
                    Welcome to the Bust Out BBS.

We offer a special FREE one week trial access to the system.  If
you are interested in trying this you must follow these steps:

1. Download MEMBER.FRM.
2. Please [J]oin conference #1 and leave a [C]omment to the sysop
   requesting the FREE trial offer.  Your request will be answered
   within 48hrs.
3. Read bulletins #1,2 and 3 or download them as BULL1, BULL2, BULL3

Our System offers a wide range of computer items and services.
The system has thousands of files over 7 gig in all.  The latest
versions of shareware and public domain software.  We have a huge
adult filebase.  We have several on-line CD-ROMs with more thousands
of new shareware and graphics files.

The system includes many world wide message networks including many
adult conferences.  We also have access to the Internet.  At your
present security level, you are allowed to access ten message and
three file areas (no adult areas).  So ask for the FREE access.
-Pause- [C]ontinue, [N]onStop? [C]
```

Figure 11.5

The welcome screen for the Bust Out BBS in California

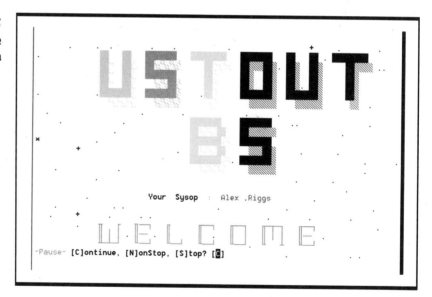

```
          Your  Sysop  :  Alex .Riggs

          W E L C O M E
-Pause- [C]ontinue, [N]onStop, [S]top? [C]
```

The main menu, shown in Figure 11.6, gives you an idea of the services available. Most bulletin boards will have some sort of central place like this.

I selected "J" to Join a Conference and got a list of conferences available (Figure 11.7)

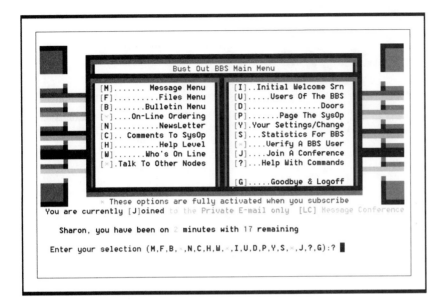

Figure 11.6

The bulletin board's main menu

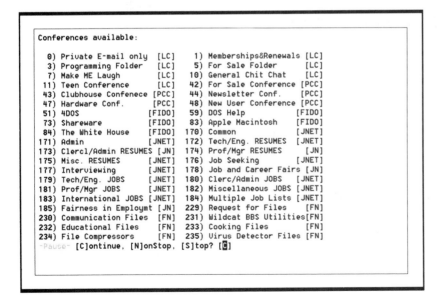

Figure 11.7

A list of the conferences available on this (relatively small) local bulletin board takes more than one full screen.

As you can see, it isn't very difficult to move around. Some bulletin boards will also give you a voice phone number to call for help. All BBSs will have a place where you can leave messages for the sysop, to get assistance or other information.

What's It Cost?

WARNING

Although most BBS operators are above board, there are still some that tolerate traffic in pirated software. Not only is this immoral, it's also dangerous, because these are the kinds of places where software is not scanned for viruses. You could easily pick up a very nasty bug this way. Don't be tempted to try to get something for nothing!

Bulletin Boards are almost always cheaper than commercial services. A goodly number are even free. The ones that offer connections to the Internet and very large libraries of software are, by and large, the most expensive, ranging up to as much as $40 per month—though most are much less.

Charges are usually so-much-per-month, but a few charge by the year.

However, almost all BBSs have limits on the amount of time you can spend online, perhaps an hour or two per day. Some have limits on the amount of shareware you can download in a day, and some have upload/download ratios. In other words, you have to contribute (upload) a certain amount of material in return for the amount of material you receive (download).

A Final Word

While not as easy to find as the big commercial systems, bulletin boards have the undeniable advantage of being considerably cheaper. Also, if you find the right bulletin board nearby, it can easily become a home away from home. You can acquire a wealth of excellent shareware, graphics, technical advice, and friendly chat, all for one very low price! It may take a bit of exploration to find them, but there are wonderful services out there to be found.

Twelve

Sending and Receiving Files

· ·

There are lots of different ways files are sent and received by computer. All the major on-line services have provisions for transmitting files from their libraries. You can also usually send files to other subscribers and receive files from them.

The process of transferring files is known as *uploading* and *downloading*. You upload a file when you send it from your computer to another computer—whether it's an on-line service, a bulletin board, or a friend in Fresno. When you transfer a file from an on-line service or a bulletin board or that friend's computer to your own computer, you're downloading it.

Why Do It ?

One reason for transferring files by modem is speed. A file sent by telephone wire is faster than even the fastest courier service. Another reason is convenience. If you send a file to a friend on CompuServe, it can be sent when you want and can be retrieved at a time that suits your friend's schedule. And, of course, file transfers give you access to programs and information files from around the globe—stuff you would have a very hard time finding any other way.

File Types

Two basic file transfer categories are offered in communications software. The two types are:

- ASCII (or text)
- Binary

ASCII transfers are possible only when the file being sent is made up exclusively of ASCII characters. If a file has the extensions .TXT or .BAT, it's probably an ASCII file.

Originally, all files that were sent back and forth on computers went via ASCII transfers. It's not a method used much any more, however, because now even the simplest word processor file usually has lots of other formatting codes (margin settings, fonts, and so forth), all of which will be lost (or worse, will cause the transfer to fail). Almost anything can screw up an ASCII file transfer, including accented characters from another language. Anything that includes a caret (^) is bound to lock up the receiving system because it's read as a flow control or other command character.

Telephone line noise will also irrevocably ding an ASCII file transfer, causing the transfer to fail, and line noise is present on every telephone system to a greater or lesser degree.

ASCII transfers lend themselves to garbling, because there isn't any error checking at all.

Binary files can contain anything in any character position. All program files, graphics, spreadsheets, and word processor files are binary.

You should always choose binary as a transfer method, because binary transfers use a reliable error-checking protocol to make sure the file is sent and received accurately. If you happen to have a large text file to transfer, binary is safest even for that, because of the built-in error checking.

NOTE

When transferring a file, a text file can be treated as binary but a binary cannot be sent as text.

How Protocols Work

A *protocol* is a set of rules determining how data is transferred. When a protocol is used, data is moved in groups of characters (called *blocks* or *packets*) that are of a fixed size. The size can range from 96 to 1024 characters or larger.

It works like this: the sending computer transmits one block at a time. The block can contain additional information besides just the characters themselves. The receiving computer adds the block to the file in which it's storing the incoming information. It also reads and acts on any information that comes with the block. Between blocks, other information is exchanged to check and verify the block's integrity. If the block is bad, it's sent again.

Many protocols have been developed over the years. Some are faster, some are better at detecting errors. They're all equally easy to use from your point of view, because their relative simplicity or complexity is hidden from view.

Both computers at either end of a file transfer must be using the same protocol. Most on-line services give you a choice of several protocols, some give you no choice at all. General telecommunications software (ProComm, Crosstalk, and so forth) will support many protocols, so you can usually find one that will work with those available on the BBS or other service you call.

Here's a brief look at some of the more popular protocols you're likely to come across.

Xmodem

The Xmodem protocol is one you're likely to encounter frequently. Designed in the late '70s and placed in the public domain, it's a standard used by virtually every system. If you get a choice of protocols when you call a BBS or an on-line service, Xmodem will surely be among them.

Xmodem transfers files in blocks of 128 bytes each. It adds an extra bit (called a *checksum*) to every block. The receiving computer uses a mathematical formula that compares the checksum with the contents of the block and verifies that the block has been accurately received. If the math doesn't work out, the transmitting computer is requested to resend the block.

Xmodem is not fast, but it's accurate and it's absolutely ubiquitous.

Ymodem

Ymodem was designed to improve on the speed of Xmodem by increasing the block size to 1,024 bytes. This increase in block size speeds transfer rates when only a few errors are encountered. However, if there's a lot of line noise, the retransmission of bad blocks slows everything down considerably.

The error-checking capability of Ymodem is just as good as Xmodem, and Ymodem is almost as widely available as Xmodem.

Kermit

Kermit is similar to Xmodem, in that it transfers files in blocks (though Kermit uses the term *packets*). Like Xmodem, it uses a checksum for error checking, but unlike Xmodem, it can recover a file transmission interrupted by line noise.

Kermit is not used by many on-line services, but its availability is growing. It's supported by the Microsoft Windows Terminal program (which also supports Xmodem). Kermit can be a little finicky and difficult to set up. Both the receiving and transmitting computers must be using the same version of Kermit for everything to work properly.

Zmodem

Zmodem is the protocol of choice these days. It's faster than Xmodem, uses larger blocks, and can resume an interrupted transfer. It's also available on almost as many services as Xmodem and Ymodem.

System-Specific Protocols

When you use software that is made for a specific on-line service, you don't need to be concerned about protocols. For example, CompuServe uses one of its own protocols (B, B Plus, or Quick B) when you transfer files using WinCIM, DOS CIM, OzCIS, or TapCIS software.

America Online and Prodigy include their own proprietary protocols in the software you use to access those services.

Which Protocol?

Generally speaking, it's a good idea to have as many protocols available in your communications software as possible, even though Xmodem and Zmodem are by far the most common. Either Xmodem or Zmodem (usually both) will be used on almost any BBS or on-line service, so you'll want to have both of those for sure.

If you're going to be dealing with a BBS or other service that offers a system-specific protocol, it's a good idea to have that protocol, too. This is good even if the system offers Xmodem or Kermit or any of the other generally-available protocols. A system's own protocol will usually be faster and more efficient on that system than any general-purpose protocol.

Transferring Files on On-Line Services

Most on-line services provide an easy way to transfer files from one subscriber to another. For example, if you're using WinCIM, you select

Send File from the Mail menu and fill in the destination and the file-name, as shown in Figure 12.1. You can then click on Send Now (for immediate delivery) or the Out-Basket (for later delivery).

Figure 12.1

Sending a file using WinCIM

On America Online, it's equally simple to transfer files. When you send an e-mail message, just click on the Attach File icon. Choose the drive, subdirectory, and filename of the file you want to send, as shown in Figure 12.2. Then just click on the Send icon, and AOL takes it from there.

Figure 12.2

You can send a file by attaching it to a message on America Online.

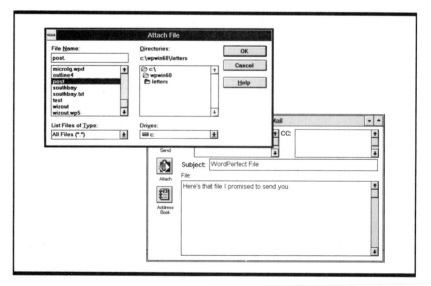

When you receive a file, it shows up as a message from the person who sent it. In the case of CompuServe, the file is copied into your CIM or WinCIM Download subdirectory. With America Online, your mail displays an icon of a $3^1/_2$-inch disk, giving you the choice of receiving the file now or later.

You can also transfer files in and out of the public areas of on-line services. To download a file from an on-line service, you first have to get to the library or database where the file is stored. This is usually done through a series of menus. You can then read the file's description and select Download from the menu or prompt that follows. Depending on the system, you may or may not be able to select a specific protocol.

Figure 12.3 shows the process of downloading a file from DELPHI. After DELPHI gives you a choice of protocols and you decide which one you want to use, ProComm for Windows takes over, showing the progress of the download.

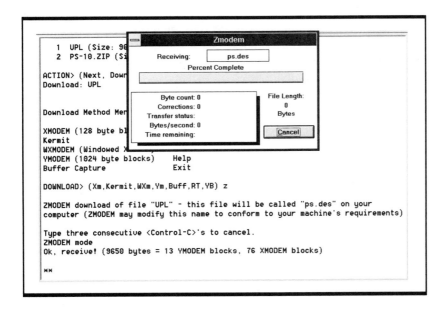

Figure 12.3

Downloading a file from the graphics database on DELPHI

Many on-line services also maintain libraries of files contributed by members. CompuServe's many forums, for example, often solicit contributions from members. You will need to consult the sysop for the individual forum or database to get the rules and restrictions on uploads.

In WinCIM, you go to the forum, then select Contribute from the Library menu. Fill in the information requested and then select OK to upload the file.

Transferring Files between Personal Computers

For most file transfers between individual computers, the best method is to simply dial the computer of the other person. Once the phone link is made, use your individual software to send and receive files.

However, establishing a successful link can be a matter of trial and error. Unless you're both using the same communications software, you'll probably have a few failed tries before you succeed. Don't be discouraged. To help in the process, try any or all of these steps:

- Make a preliminary voice call to establish the communications parameters you'll be using (such as bps rate) and to confirm that you'll both be using the same data, parity, and stop bits.
- Type a few lines back and forth before you try to transmit a file to make sure the communication link is stable.
- Try transmitting a small test file before you jump in to send a multi-megabyte monster.

If the two of you are fortunate enough to be using the same communications program, you can usually make your connection without a problem. For example, I often exchange files with a friend who uses ProComm Plus (for DOS). Using my ProComm for Windows, I dial his computer. The connection is made automatically with the two programs deciding between themselves how to do things, and all I have to provide is the name of the file and the protocol I want to use. The file transfer takes place without either human having to contribute any thought to the process. (Needless to say, this is the preferred method.)

Transferring Files on a BBS

Most BBSs make provisions for uploading and downloading files from public areas. Either there'll be a database entry on the main menu of the BBS or, in the case of larger BBSs, the databases will be inside the special interest group areas.

To download a file, you usually select from a list, as shown in Figure 12.4. The list will often show how long it takes to download the file and how many times the file has been downloaded by others. You select the download command from a menu, specify a protocol if requested, enter the filename, and start your system's download procedure when prompted.

Uploading is also fairly simple. You select Upload from a menu. The system then prompts you for a filename and a brief description of the file, and generally takes care of the process from there on. A file you upload may be immediately placed in the database, but it will more likely be stored temporarily until the sysop has a chance to review it and, in the case of a program file, scan it for viruses.

 NOTE

Some BBSs ask you to select a default protocol at the time you join up. Thereafter, you won't be prompted to select a protocol when you download or upload files.

Figure 12.4
Some of the files available for download from a BBS

```
Dwnlds: 0       DL Time   00:03:55

TRIPPLAN.ZIP  105,435   09/29/93 | Vacation planner.  Plans your auto trip
Dwnlds: 3       DL Time   00:01:08 | for you with maps,

ZULU.EXE      220,544   08/31/93 | ZULU Amateur Radio Log Book.
Dwnlds: 0       DL Time   00:02:23 |

HOMEINUT.ZIP  300,836   09/22/93 | Home Inventory program.  Very good for
Dwnlds: 1       DL Time   00:03:15 | Insurance

MM707.ZIP     186,367   09/22/93 | Meal Master Recipe program.  Organize,
Dwnlds: 2       DL Time   00:02:01 | search, etc.

BACS_SER.TXT    7,851   10/31/93 | Description of Bay Area Computer
Dwnlds: 46      DL Time   00:00:05 F Services                      *Info*

BULL1           5,112   10/31/93 | Why subscribe to a BBS?
Dwnlds: 236     DL Time   00:00:03 F

BULL2           2,279   10/15/93 | How to subscribe to the Bust Out BBS
Dwnlds: 323     DL Time   00:00:01 F

BULL3           1,561   10/15/93 | Explanation fo the various access
Dwnlds: 284     DL Time   00:00:01 F levels
```

A Final Note

Electronic file transfer is one of the best reasons for having a modem. It's fast, it's convenient, and it's usually cheaper than conventional means of transmission.

Even if you're not one of the millions of people working at home, sending files to and from a central office, file transfers can be of use to you. You can acquire games, programs, and information from a local bulletin board or from a remote computer on the Internet, thousands of miles away. Especially when you're paying an on-line service by the minute, downloading a file so you can read and examine it at your convenience can save lots of money.

Part Four

Taking Care of Business

• •

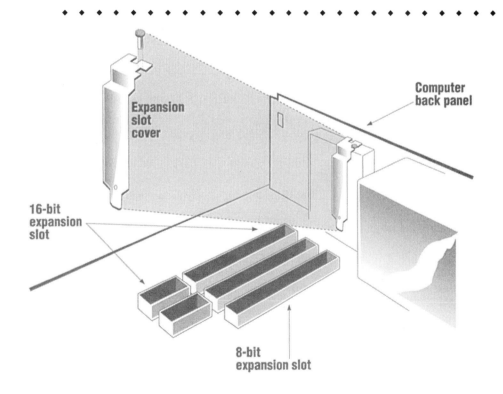

Expansion slot cover

Computer back panel

16-bit expansion slot

8-bit expansion slot

Thirteen

E-Mail and Remote Computing

• •

I f you're going to be using your modem as part of your business operations, you may be interested in a specialty electronic mail service as well as the ability to hook your out-of-office computer up to an in-office computer.

In this chapter we'll go over some of the options available to you when it comes to e-mail, and how to use your computer at the office even when you're not *in* the office.

Electronic Mail

This section actually should be called "*Other* Electronic Mail" because e-mail is part-and-parcel of virtually every service already discussed in this book.

"Dedicated" e-mail services, such as MCI Mail and SprintLink, are used almost exclusively by businesses these days. MCI Mail used to be more generally popular because your MCI Mail account number (with a prefix) was also your Telex number.

Remember Telex? ...I thought not.

Telex is another term for teletype machines. These used to be the only way to get printed material from here to there very quickly. Now that Telex machines have been eclipsed by faxes, that's not such an advantage.

So why would you want to subscribe to a specialized e-mail service? For the individual or small business, there's very little reason.

If you belong to CompuServe or any of the other major on-line services, you can already send mail to anyone with an Internet address (which includes most other on-line services and many bulletin boards) and to practically all the e-mail services, including MCI Mail, AT&TMail, and SprintMail.

 NOTE

The big on-line services, like CompuServe and America Online, will also (for a price) send your messages via fax or the U.S. Postal Service.

My recommendation is to invest in just one on-line service that has a broad range of features. That way you can send e-mail to people who are on any number of services, including people on only MCI Mail or SprintMail. You'll also have the added bonus of *receiving* all your mail in one location, so you don't have to call around to four or five different places to get your messages.

If you don't want to do that, you can get a dedicated e-mail service. Here are brief descriptions of the major companies that provide specialized e-mail services.

MCI Mail

MCI Mail is probably still the biggest player among the specialized mail services. The recent growth of the X.400 addressing system has enabled MCI Mail to expand its connections to 52 mail systems in 40 countries.

What's This X.400 Address Thing?

Somewhere in every e-mail system you'll come across a reference to X.400 addresses. X.400 is another idea that came from those same wonderful folks (the CCITT) who brought us V.32 and V.42bis and other such stuff.

The CCITT X.400 recommendations consist of 600 pages of protocols and procedures that define a global scheme for electronic mail. The overall name for the X.400 recommendations is Message Handling Systems (MHS), which is why you'll also see the term "MHS Gateway" attached to various services.

Every mail system that subscribes to these rules and regulations has an X.400 address. If you know someone with an X.400 address, you'll undoubtedly be able to send mail to that address. If you belong to CompuServe or another on-line service, you also *have* an X.400 address. You'll have to check the help files of your on-line service to get the particulars—what your X.400 address is and how to send mail to someone with an X.400 address.

If all you need is mail service, MCI Mail is a good option. It's not expensive, it connects to virtually every other service and it offers a number of extra features. With MCI Mail, you can:

- Send mail by Telex, by U.S. Postal Service, or by fax as well as by the usual electronic transfer

- Register your signature, and MCI Mail will attach it to paper or other transmissions as you request
- Register your letterhead, and MCI Mail will print your paper mail on it
- Send an instant message (the recipient is called and notified of a message in their mailbox)
- Connect directly to the Dow Jones News/Retrieval Service

MCI Mail can be a bargain, too. In most parts of the U.S., you can access MCI Mail through no-charge 800 numbers. MCI Mail offers a Preferred Pricing plan that's just $10 per month, and for that ten bucks, you can send up to 40 messages per month (e-mail or domestic fax).

AT&TMail

At&TMail, which is also AT&T's own internal mail system, is a product that aims solely at the corporate customer, especially at companies that want to integrate their computing and telecommunications packages. It provides full e-mail service and a pricing structure that favors the large-volume user.

One unique feature of AT&T Mail is Mail Talk, which allows you to retrieve your messages by phone. A sophisticated voice synthesizer not only reads your mail to you, but also provides on-line help.

SprintMail

SprintMail is another service meant primarily for corporate users. The main disadvantage of SprintMail is that it's completely command driven—that means no nice, friendly menus or dialog boxes.

On the other hand, SprintMail is fast and offers a lot of features in addition to the usual paper mail, fax, and telex services, for example:

- Access to the NewsGrid news service, the Official Airline Guide, and the Dow Jones News/Retrieval Service
- Binary file upload, download, and transfer
- Access to a large number of special bulletin boards created by companies and organizations that use the service

Because SprintMail is owned by SprintNet (the telephone network people), it has direct access to more countries of the world than most services. However, since everybody now has connections to the world of X.400 addresses, that's less of an advantage than it was a few years ago.

Other Players

In addition to the above-named companies, there are a zillion other e-mail services—such as InfoNet, Advantis (AKA The IBM Mail Exchange), AppleLink, GEnie, EasyLink, the electronic mail service run by Germany's Deutsche Bundesposte (DBP), and heaven knows what else. If you have a lot of friends and/or business contacts on one of these services, it may pay you to join that one directly.

For most people, however, the best e-mail solution will be whatever on-line service you find comfortable. Join CompuServe or DELPHI or America Online for the features they offer and get full e-mail service thrown in as a bonus.

Remote Computing

With the addition of the right kind of software, you can use your modem to connect to another computer (also equipped with a modem and the same software). You can then use the remote computer as if you were actually sitting in front of it. In this way, you can call your computer at home from the office and, as long as the computer at home is turned on, download or upload files without the intervention of another human.

Or, if you are working at home, you can call the computer at the office and run a program that isn't even on your home computer. For example, from your home computer, you can start up QuattroPro on the office computer, load in a spreadsheet, and see the data on your monitor at home!

Why Not Just Transfer Files?

Using remote control software may seem like overkill. After all, you can just call up the modem on your office computer and transfer files back and forth. True. But when you do that, you will have limitations on what you can accomplish.

Let's say you want something that's on the file server on the LAN (local area network) that your office computer is a part of. If you use the remote software to sign on to your office computer, the office computer can go get the file you want from the file server at a speed much faster than your modem can transmit. You can then look at or change the file without having to spend the time to transmit it to your home computer.

What if you want to use or change a file that belongs to a program you don't even have on your hard disk at home? You could download the file, but then you wouldn't be able to load it on the home computer. With remote computing software, you can sign on to the remote computer from wherever you are and run the program on the remote computer, load the file in question, change it over the phone line, and save it, again on the remote computer.

Of course, if the remote computer is on a network, the network administrator will have to set things up so that you can have access and still maintain the network's security.

 NOTE

Unlike other types of software, remote computing programs are designed to be installed on more than one machine at a time.

A number of programs are available to do this kind of trickery. My personal favorite, called pcANYWHERE, is made by Symantec. (Other programs, such as Carbon Copy Plus or PC Commute, work similarly.) pcANYWHERE is available in DOS and Windows versions and is simplicity itself to use.

First, install it on each computer you'll be using it with (the one at home and the one at the office, for example). As you install, you'll be instructed to give each computer a name. You may be whimsical if you want, but the name should be one you'll remember.

After the software is installed, click on the pcANYWHERE icon to start the program. You set one computer up to be the host (that's the one that gets called) by selecting the Be a Host PC button. The first time you set up a host, you have to configure the host options as shown in Figure 13.1. After that first time, when you select Be a Host PC, you get the more simplified screen shown in Figure 13.2. After everything's complete, click on Wait for Call.

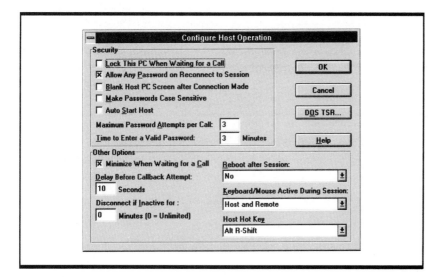

Figure 13.1

Setting up the host computer the first time

The pcANYWHERE program will shrink to an icon at the bottom of the screen with the legend: "Waiting…" as shown in Figure 13.3.

Leave the computer turned on. You can turn off the monitor, but the computer should be *on* (and in the case of pcANYWHERE for Windows, Windows should be left running, too). Now the host computer is ready and waiting for that moment when you call it from another location.

Figure 13.2

Setting up the host computer
subsequently

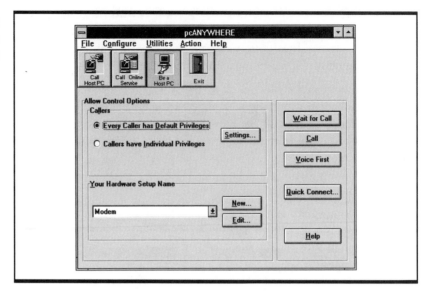

Figure 13.3

ANYWHERE loaded on a host
computer and "Waiting…"

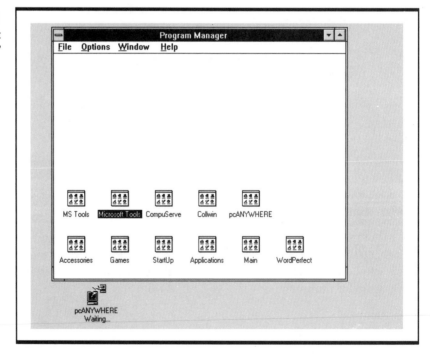

When you want to call the host computer, start pcANYWHERE on the other computer and click on the Call Host PC button (Figure 13.4).

Click on the Edit button so you can provide information about the phone number, the host computer's name (you *do* remember the name, don't you?), and so forth (Figure 13.5).

You may have to use the Edit button under Hardware Selection, too, to make sure the program knows where your modem is (COM1, COM2) and what the correct transmission rate is (9600, 14,400).

Now all you have to do is click on the Call button and connect with the host computer.

Is it really that easy? Well, probably not. Like all other direct modem-to-modem connections (that don't involve a big on-line service) it may take some tinkering and trial-and-error to get things working right. But this isn't brain surgery, after all, and if you run into trouble, you can always click on that Call Online Service button (Figure 13.6). From there you can call directly to the Symantec BBS and get technical support.

 NOTE

This is one time that very fast modems can be a lot of help. Even if your V.Fast or V.32terbo can't communicate to more typical modems at a rate faster than 14.4kbps, if you have a V.Fast or V.32terbo modem at either end of a remote computing operation, you'll get V(ery)Fast results indeed.

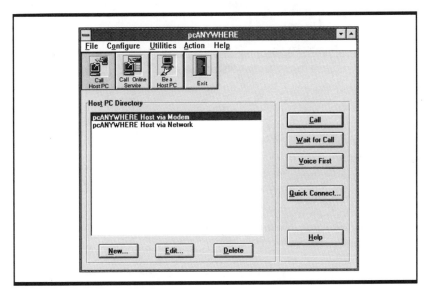

Figure 13.4

Getting ready to call the host computer

Figure 13.5

The information you need to
provide so you can call the
host computer

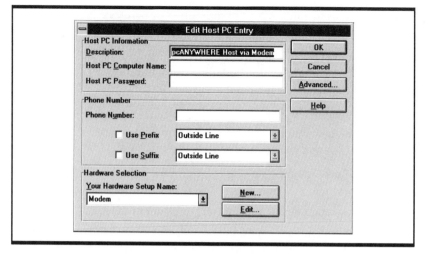

Figure 13.6

A connection to Symantec's
bulletin board is already
built in.

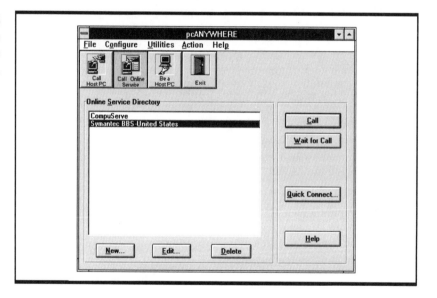

Bear in mind that even a not-very-fast hard disk will transfer information to your active memory at 700-800Kb per second. The fastest modem is very slow compared to that. However, all the remote computing programs use clever data-compression techniques and other tricks to make the operation as transparent and fast as possible, so the apparent speed (as you work) is fairly tolerable, but it won't ever be as fast as working at your own local computer.

Remote computing software can also be used to transfer files between two computers without using a modem at all. Let's say you want to move files from your laptop to your desktop, or vice versa. Just connect the two machines using a null modem cable (no modem required) and the software will let you move the files without resorting to floppies. (Consult the documentation for full details.)

A Final Note

Specialized e-mail services and remote computing are not for everyone, but they are options you should know about. For many business users, an e-mail service may provide enough features for all occasions. You may not need the forums, recreational, and research facilities offered by the big on-line services, particularly if most of your business contacts have accounts on one e-mail service or another. In that case, being a "resident" on that same service may give you easier access to these people in a shorter amount of time.

For business travelers (or those who like to work at home occasionally), remote computing software may enable you to keep in touch with what's going on in ways that can't be replicated easily by other methods. Investigate the various remote computing packages and make sure to get one that will work with the equipment you have. If one of the computers concerned is on a network, you'll need to involve the network administrator in the choice and installation of the software, but in general, remote computing software is remarkably easy both to set up and to use.

Fourteen

Faxes and Voice Mail

• •

In two recent developments in modem communications, fax and voice mail capabilities are included right in the hardware.

Fax modems started being available a few years ago. Like most computer "breakthroughs," this one had a rocky beginning. Early users found they could send faxes but not receive them (or vice versa). The software was buggy and the hardware unreliable. Thanks to the pioneering work of both those who made the fax modems and those who struggled to use them, fax modems are now both commonplace and easy to use—especially with Windows.

187

Voice mail capability is now about where fax modems were three years ago. Some modems with built-in voice mail are still finicky to set up and have real limitations in their use, but it won't be long before they catch up.

Voice mail systems are discussed later in this chapter. First we'll deal with the fax part of the fax modem system.

A Brief History of Fax

Practically everybody remembers a time, just a few years ago, when faxes were rare. Now it's rare to find an office in America without at least one fax machine.

Facsimile transmissions actually have been around for a long time—the original patent for a fax-type device was issued in 1842. Newspaper wire photos have been sent all over the globe for decades, too, using the same basic idea of employing an electro-mechanical device to translate wire-based signals into marks on paper.

The widespread use of faxes in business began about the time desktop computers appeared on the scene. But even desktop computers didn't take off until a standard was set: the IBM PC. Similarly, faxes exploded in popularity only after the CCITT adopted transmission standards.

The first two standards, Group 1 and Group 2, were analog in nature and therefore very slow. The fastest Group 2 fax takes three minutes to transmit a page!

In 1980, the CCITT approved the Group 3 standard, which led to the current explosion in faxes. The Group 3 standard is entirely digital. It uses data compression and modems up to 9600bps, which means a document can be sent at a rate of 30–60 seconds per page. About 90 percent of the world's fax devices are Group-3-compatible.

A newer standard, Group 4, was approved in 1984. On the plus side, this standard allows the sending of material using a resolution of 400 dots per inch (dpi), as contrasted to Group 3's maximum resolution of 200 dpi. Unfortunately, the first Group 4 machines required high-speed, dedicated phone lines, so they didn't catch on. Newer Group 4 faxes are emerging that are also compatible with Group 3 machines, but they're still expensive and they are not widely available.

Fax Modems and Fax Machines

A fax (short for *facsimile*) is, in it's simplest terms, a modem for pictures. A fax board or (machine) converts images (graphics or *text*) into a series of lines and all the lines into a continuous string of information. At the receiving end, the data stream is converted into dots, duplicating the pattern of the original. It doesn't matter if the original page contains graphics or text, the fax sees it all as a graphic image.

Whether you're using a freestanding fax machine or the fax part of the fax modem inside your computer, the process is very similar. For a fax machine the steps are:

1. You stick a piece of paper in the machine. An electronic image of the document is made using a device inside the fax machine called a *scanner*. The scanner works much like a copy machine except that it makes a binary electronic image instead of a paper copy.

2. A special kind of modem translates the binary information to analog signals that can be transmitted over a phone line to a receiving device.

3. The receiving fax machine's modem turns the analog signals back into binary ones. It then reproduces the original document by, in effect, reversing the scanning process of the sending machine. The receiving machine then prints out the document.

When you send a document using a fax modem, the steps are:

1. You start with either a PC-created image or one that was imported from a freestanding scanner—in either case, the document will be electronic (binary), not paper.

2. The modem part of the fax modem translates the binary signals into analog ones and sends them over the phone line.

3. The receiving modem converts the signals back to binary form and then hands them over to the fax software.

4. At this point, the document is displayed on the monitor or printed on a standard printer. (You can also just store the image on your hard disk to look at it later.)

As you can see, the differences are slight, but depending on your needs, they can be significant. For example, if you receive faxes that you want to be able to edit and return, a fax modem is what you need. On the other hand, if most of what you fax out is clippings, documents, or forms that are *not* created inside your PC, a freestanding fax machine is your ticket.

I've participated in many a discussion on this topic and have come to the conclusion that there's no perfect solution…yet. Table 14.1 shows what's easy and what's difficult in each set up. For my part, I've opted for an inclusive (but fairly expensive) combination of a fax modem and a peripheral scanner. It's not the cheapest solution, but it does cover all contingencies.

If you've bought a modem recently, you probably have fax capability anyway, so it's not a choice between a fax modem and a fax machine. Depending on your usage, you may well find the fax modem to be all you need. On the other hand, a separate fax machine or a scanner may also be necessary (or at least desirable).

What You Want to Do	Solution with a Fax Modem	Solution with a Freestanding Fax Machine
Send documents created on your computer	Transmit directly, using the fax modem	Print out on a printer, then transmit
Send forms or other documents that didn't come from your computer	Scan in to make a computer document, then transmit using the fax modem	Transmit directly, using the fax machine
Make a few copies	Scan the original, using a separate scanning device, then print it out on your printer	Use the fax machine's scanner and print it out on thermal paper (which curls and fades), or buy and use a plain-paper fax machine
Convert a faxed document into a computer-read-able text file	Use OCR software to translate the fax into a computer file	No can do (unless you also have a separate scanner attached to your computer)

Table 14.1

Fax modems versus fax machines

Fax Software

Your fax modem probably came equipped with some sort of fax software. Like the software that comes with the modem, this software may be quite minimalist. If you do much in the way of faxing, you'll want to look at some of the bigger fax software packages that offer features such as:

Dialing directories   Files in which you can store lists of individuals and groups so you can send faxes without entering numbers manually.

NOTE

The best way to do background faxing is with a combination of hardware (a fax board with a built-in coprocessor chip) and software. A software-only solution can be used, but it's much more likely to noticeably slow down the computer, especially if you're running processor-intensive software such as graphics or CAD programs. Being able to send and receive faxes in the background is an invaluable feature if you do much faxing at all. It means you can go on with your other work instead of drumming your fingers on the desktop waiting for that interminable document to be sent (or received).

◎ **TIP**

Fax alert is especially helpful if you have a fax modem that receives faxes in the background. In that case, you don't hear the arrival of a fax (no phone ringing, no loud connect noises), so you can easily not notice that a fax has come in until several days later when you receive an irate phone call from the sender asking why you haven't responded.

Scheduled transmissions   A time you can set for unattended document sending, for example, late at night when lines are less busy and phone rates are lower.

Polling   An operation in which one fax calls another and requests and receives a specific stored file.

Background operation   The ability of the software (or hardware) to receive or send a fax while you're doing something else on the computer.

Automatic callback   The automatic calling back of busy numbers (some software will also try an alternate number).

Prefixes and suffixes   The ability to specify a prefix of *70 (to disable Call Waiting) or 9 (to get an outside line), so you won't have to type it in at every entry.

Graphics conversion   This option translates graphics files received by fax into formats used by specific graphics or desktop publishing programs.

Optical character recognition (OCR)   A program that translates a fax, which is a *picture* of a document, into actual text files that you can then edit on your word processor.

Scan and fax   An option that lets you scan in a document and fax it out to a recipient in one step (a necessary feature if you have a scanner).

Annotation   The option to mark up a fax before you file it, fax it back or pass it on.

Fax alert   A pop-up window that lets you know when a fax has been received.

Cover sheets and page headers   The pages or headings (some will be provided, or you can design your own) that identify outgoing documents.

Check out any software package thoroughly before you buy to make sure it does what you want it to do.

The Inside Story on Software

One of the standard ways to find software you like is to ask around. But what if your friends don't use fax software? What if you're the one *they* ask for help?

A great place to research software (or hardware too, for that matter) is the world of on-line services. CompuServe, in particular, has an enormous range of forums devoted to technical support; America Online and Prodigy also have large areas.

Sign on to an on-line service and see if the software manufacturer has a presence in a forum or on a bulletin board. Read a few days' worth of messages on the subject of the software you're considering buying. Bearing in mind that usually the only people who come to a technical support forum are those who are having some sort of problem, notice what kinds of difficulties those people are bringing up. Do they appear to generally like the software? Or are they flaming mad because they feel ripped off?

You can also determine a lot about the company from how their representatives deal with the problems. The company reps are, after all, the ones who set the tone for the forum. Are they quick to respond or do messages languish unanswered for days at a time? Are they friendly or just barely polite? Are their solutions helpful or confusing? This is the place you may go for answers to questions after you buy. Will you feel comfortable asking a question here?

Of course, this is not a complete substitute for reading up on the subject in magazines and other publications, but it can show you a side of the software you're not likely to learn about from any other source.

Top Choices in Fax Software

The best fax software packages are made to be used in Windows. The reason I like these is that they don't require that you have anything resembling brains in order to use them. You just install them after your fax modem is installed, and you're ready to send and receive faxes. You may have to look in the documentation to figure out some of the more advanced features, but for the basic stuff, no research is required.

Another reason Windows programs are best is because fax programs are installed as TSR (terminate-and-stay-resident) programs. Windows handles this type of program much better than DOS alone does. With DOS, you're much more likely to have a conflict among programs that may then take some effort to sort out. With Windows programs, you have a good chance of getting everything working together without a lot of grief.

WinFax

 TIP

WinFax comes with macros that add WinFax to the File menus of Word for Windows, Microsoft Excel, and Ami Pro. If you install these macros, you no longer have to select WinFax as a printer. You can keep your regular printer and just choose WinFax when you have a fax to send out.

Made by Delrina Corporation, WinFax has been around for a number of years but has become the best-selling fax program only in its current incarnation: WinFax Pro 3.0. This is the Cadillac of fax programs. It's big (7MB of hard disk space required), and has lots of bells, whistles, and fancy trimmings. WinFax has everything you're ever likely to need and a lot of stuff you'll probably never use. If you're the sort of person who wants the top-of-the-line version of everything, this is the program for you. The retail price for WinFax Pro is $129, though you can easily find it available by mail order at $80 or a bit less.

Using WinFax Pro to send faxes is a no-brainer. Just open the document you want. The Windows application that the document's in will have a Printer Select or Printer Setup item, probably in the File menu. Figure 14.1 shows the dialog box you get when you choose Select Printer in WordPerfect for Windows. Figure 14.2 shows what the dialog box looks like in Paradox for Windows.

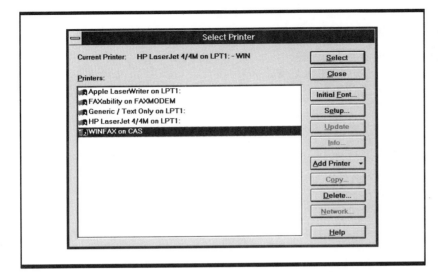

Figure 14.1

To fax a document from WordPerfect for Windows, select WinFax as a printer.

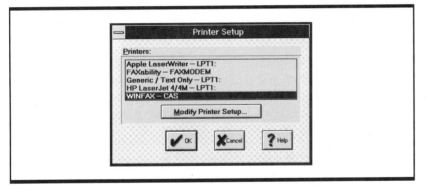

Figure 14.2

To fax a document from Paradox for Windows, choose WinFax as the destination for the file.

Once WinFax is selected as the "printer," print the file as you would ordinarily do. WinFax will open up so you can then tell it to whom the fax should be sent. You don't have to do anything to receive a file—other than have your computer on—because WinFax has a TSR that'll let you receive a fax even when you're out of Windows and working in the DOS environment.

WinFax comes complete with a whole book full of fax cover pages to choose from, which is one of the reasons the program takes up so much hard-disk room. The cover sheets do give your faxes some punch, though, as you can see from the example in Figure 14.3.

Figure 14.3

One of WinFax's fax cover sheets

WinFax will send and receive faxes in the Windows background. It doesn't require a modem with a coprocessor and doesn't slow the computer down too much. To enable background sending, you have to open Program Setup (as shown in Figure 14.4) from the Fax menu.

Figure 14.4

The Program Setup dialog box in WinFax

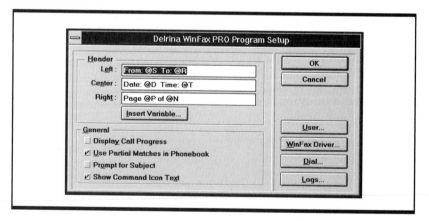

Remove the checkmark next to Display Call Progress and then when you send a fax you can go on with your other work undisturbed. To set what's in the header of each page, click on Insert Variable. A list of things you can include will appear (Figure 14.5).

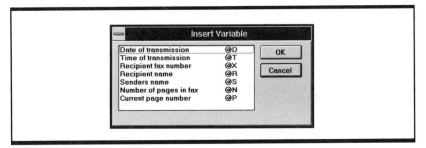

Figure 14.5
The items that can be included in headers

WinFax has very sophisticated tools for annotating faxes, and a fairly good program for cleaning up those faxes that arrive with miscellaneous "line noise" markings on them.

WinFax includes an OCR program in the package. It's not especially good and it's not especially fast. It'll do, however, if your OCR requirements are minimal. If someone sends you a nice, clear fax at high resolution in a non-fancy font, you'll probably be able to read it in the OCR program with very few errors. But an alarmingly high number of faxes are not clear. And if it was sent on a manually-fed fax machine and it's just a little bit askew, you're out of luck.

In general, WinFax is a program rich in features and possibilities. A visit to the Delrina forum on CompuServe confirms that the program can be finicky to set up and operate. Lots of people have a variety of problems. On the other hand, Delrina tech support, which used to be famously cavalier, seems to have improved. However, I can't honestly recommend WinFax Pro unless you have to have every possible feature *and* you don't mind a program that resembles a Jaguar as much as a Cadillac (i.e., it's very luxe, but spends way too much time not working).

 **WARNING**
The OCR program with WinFax requires 4.5MB of ROM just to run. Don't even try unless you have at least 6MB installed.

Eclipse Fax

Eclipse is a modestly-sized package (less than 1MB in hard-drive space required) that has a full list of features that also work very well. Like all

Windows fax programs, Eclipse makes sending and receiving faxes easy. You just select EFax as the printer and then print the document.

Eclipse's Send Fax dialog box (Figure 14.6) is very easy to figure out. As you can see in the lower-right corner of the dialog box, you can preview a fax before you send it, mark it up (annotate it), place an image on the fax, and append pages. In each case, when you check one or more of these boxes, the program steps you through the process.

Figure 14.6

The Send Fax dialog box in Eclipse Fax

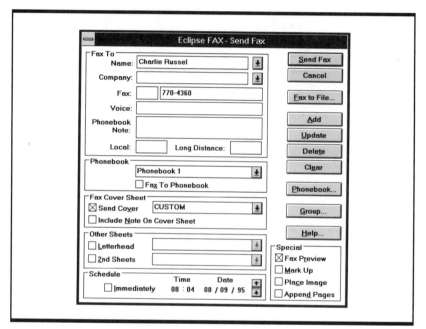

Eclipse is particularly good at cleaning up less-than-perfect incoming faxes. Figure 14.7 shows a fax before clean up. Figure 14.8 shows the same fax after Eclipse's Clear View was used on it. I don't know if the Eclipse OCR program is absolutely the best, but I am sure it's the best program for under $100 (the list price is $129, but you can find Eclipse advertised in many catalogs for about $70). The OCR program is very fast and makes fewer errors than either WinFax Pro or Faxability Plus/OCR.

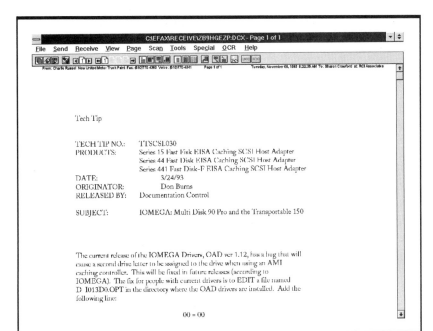

Figure 14.7

An incoming fax, as received

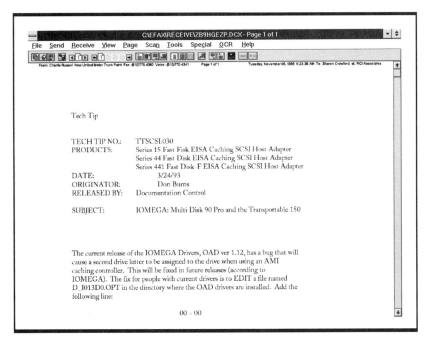

Figure 14.8

The same fax after Eclipse's Clear View was used to clean it up

Eclipse's background processing is quick and unobtrusive. You can also organize your faxes, both incoming and outgoing, and schedule transmissions for other times. In general, Eclipse is a bargain, because it does all the fancy stuff while remaining easy to use at the basic level.

Faxability Plus

I'm very partial to Faxability Plus, mainly because it works so well with my Intel modem. In fact, if you have an Intel fax modem, Faxability is the only reasonable choice. Because they're made by the same company, the Intel fax modem and the Intel software understand each other perfectly. The Faxability software often comes free when you buy an Intel modem. But be aware that there are two versions: one with OCR and one without. Don't get the wrong one by mistake. If you don't get it free with the modem, Faxability Plus with OCR costs about $80. Without OCR, it's around $55.

With Faxability Plus, you send faxes in the standard way: by choosing the fax modem as your printer. Faxes arrive silently and in the background, even if your modem doesn't have the expensive coprocessor (those in the SatisFAXtion line). If it *does* have the coprocessor, receiving or sending a fax will be invisible, regardless of whatever else you might be doing at the time.

When you choose the print command from your application, the window shown in Figure 14.9 opens. Various options (shown in Figure 14.10) are set by clicking on the options button. You can include a cover sheet or not, select a logo for the cover sheet, and so forth.

If you get the version of Faxability with OCR, you'll get a very good character recognition program. It can read your incoming fax into a variety of word processing formats.

Faxability doesn't have quite as many shiny features as WinFax, but it appeals to me because it works faster with an Intel modem than any other program and I have never had the slightest difficulty getting it to work.

 NOTE

Under most circumstances, it makes more sense to transmit a document as a modem-to-modem file than as a fax. If I have a WordPerfect document and send it to you by modem, you can import it into WordPerfect (or virtually any other word processor) and be sure that you're not missing a single character. With OCR software, you usually have to do a lot of proofreading for errors which, with a large file, can be time-consuming and tedious.

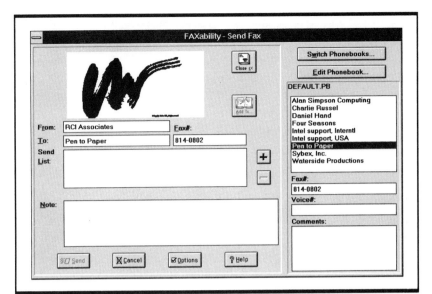

Figure 14.9
Faxability's Send Fax window

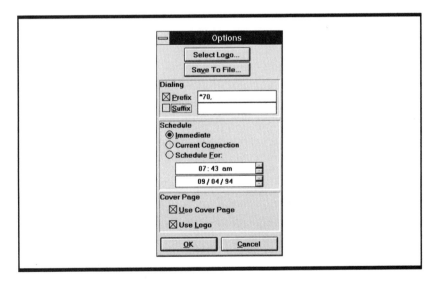

Figure 14.10
Setting the options in Faxability

WordPerfect 6 for DOS

NOTE
WordPerfect assembles its fax phone list from whatever other fax program you have on your computer.

In what's likely to be a wave of the future, WordPerfect now includes fax capability inside its new software. If you use WordPerfect for DOS, this is a perfect way to send out documents. You just select Print/Fax from the File menu and then click on Fax Services. WordPerfect opens a window, shown in Figure 14.11.

Figure 14.11
The WordPerfect fax phone book

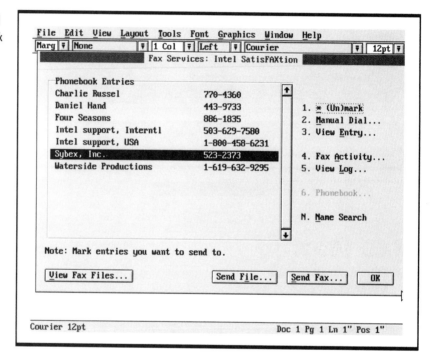

Click on Send Fax and you'll get the screen shown in Figure 14.12. As you can see, you can make a lot of the same choices available in the specialized fax programs.

WordPerfect's fax functions aren't a substitute for regular fax software. After all, you still need a program for *receiving* faxes. But it is handy, and more programs obviously will be incorporating direct fax sending in the future.

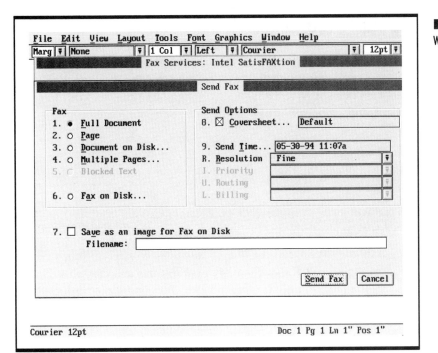

Figure 14.12
WordPerfect's fax option screen

Voice Mail

The new thing-that-costs-money appearing on the horizon is voice mail capability for your computer. If you've overheard any of the discussions about what a pain it is to get your fax modem to work reliably with an answering machine, you'll know why there's such a demand for something that will let you do all-in-one. If you have a home office, for example, you probably will need to solve this problem, unless you want to invest in a separate phone line just for the fax and modem.

Two solutions available today are the TyIN 2000 and the Ultima Home Office. Both can be found for under $200. These two products are combinations of hardware and Windows-based software that unite to keep straight all the things you do over a phone line.

TyIN 2000

The TyIN 2000 package contains an internal circuit board that goes inside your computer box just like an ordinary internal modem. The software that comes with it manages incoming phone calls for you. Fax, modem, and voice calls are all directed to the appropriate places.

The voice calls can go to any number of voice mailboxes you set up. The messages are date- and time-stamped and they can can be retrieved remotely. (Of course, you can always pick up the phone and *answer* a voice call.)

Fax features include on-screen viewing and rotation, group faxing, auto-redial, multiple phone books, and automatic cover sheets.

TyIN 2000 doesn't have as many fax features as WinFax or Eclipse, and it doesn't include OCR, but the voice mail features are a big plus. Unfortunately, the modem only transmits data at 2400bps, but that doesn't seem to faze TyIN's many devoted fans.

NOTE

Coming soon is the TyIN 4000, which will include 14.4Kbps modem capability and additional bells, whistles, and other features. This one could be very good.

Ultima Home Office

There are actually two versions of Home Office: the Home Office and the Ultima Home Office. The Ultima is the better one—its maximum modem speed is 14.4Kbps, and the fax both sends and receives at 9600bps (the regular Home Office has a maximum modem speed of 2400bps).

It has lots of the usual fax features, including some neat cover sheets. The voice mail system is easy to set up and it sounds very good to those calling in.

In general, this is a very slick package. For about $170, you can turn your phone chores over to the Ultima Home Office and make your small business sound very professional.

A Final Note

As usual, the answer to the question *what do you need* comes down to *what do you need to do*. If you don't use the fax part of your fax modem very much, you don't really need anything beyond whatever software came with the fax modem itself.

If you use your fax modem a lot, you'll want a package such as Eclipse or WinFax to add the most flexibility and maximum functionality to your fax modem.

If you have a home office, one of the voice mail packages can combine the best of all worlds for you.

One thing you can be sure of: the technology is changing so rapidly that if there's something you want and you can't find it, you can just wait a month or two and look again. It's bound to be available soon.

Fifteen

Common Problems and Their Solutions

• •

Although modems and the related communications software have improved dramatically in recent years, problems can still occur. It's an unfortunate fact of life that you're more likely to have problems with an off-brand, cheapie modem than one made by a major manufacturer. You'll usually get less tech support, too. But even with the top-of-the-line models, difficulties can happen. (An even more unfortunate fact of life: money can buy you a lot but not complete immunity from trouble.)

Problems That Aren't Problems at All

Hassles with modems fall into one of three categories:

- Hardware
- Software
- Wetware (that's you)

Many on-line problems are not problems at all, but are the result of not understanding how to use a particular system. Before you sign on, familiarize yourself with whatever materials the service provides, such as a manual or command reference sheet. Then, before you start, you should:

- Make sure the modem is connected to the phone line and, if it's external, to the computer and to its own power supply
- If the modem has a power switch, turn it on
- Make sure all communications settings in your software are correct for the system you're calling
- Make sure you're using the proper dial-up procedure
- Make sure you're using the right telephone number, system ID, and password

If you experience a problem during sign-on or while you're online, don't panic. Most communications software has either a hang-up button or a disconnect menu item. Just select that item and you'll be disconnected. Then you can try again. Different on-line services and different bulletin boards work differently. On some bulletin boards, I've had to call half a dozen times before I got the hang of it, but eventually I've been able to connect to every place I've called.

Problems with Getting Started

This section is about the difficulties you can have getting the modem to fire up and actually operate.

External modem is turned on but doesn't respond

You've flipped the modem's switch to ON, but nothing happens. The light(s) on the front of the modem may also be on.

Probable cause: If none of the lights on the front of the modem come on, it's probably not plugged in to the power source. If the lights are on, then the modem cables are either loose (more likely) or defective (fairly unlikely).

Solution: If the modem has worked before, make sure the cable is securely connected to the modem and to your COM (serial) port. If the problem persists, check the troubleshooting section of your modem's manual. You may have to run the modem diagnostics program (which is not as difficult as it sounds). That will determine if there's a defect in the modem.

Your new software won't recognize the modem

You've bought a new software package (or upgraded from an earlier version) and now your perfectly good modem refuses to function.

Probable cause: When you install new software, you frequently have to choose your modem from a list of modems that the software provides. If your modem is a year or two old, the initialization string that the software provides to use with your brand of modem may no longer work.

Solution: Contact the modem manufacturer's tech support. They will either supply you with a new initialization string (the band-aid approach) or a new ROM BIOS chip (the real solution).

The modem responds, but there's no dial tone

When you start your communications program, you can see the proper sequence of messages on your screen and maybe even hear the modem click on, but then there's not a dial tone.

Probable cause: There's a problem with the wiring in the modem itself, between the modem and the wall, or in the wall.

Solution: Check the phone wire from the modem to the wall jack. Is it connected?

If it's connected, unplug the wire from the modem and plug it into a phone that you know works. Get a dial tone? If yes, you have a modem problem.

If you get no dial tone, take the phone wire and the phone and plug into a different wall jack. Get a dial tone? If yes, the problem's in the wall jack. If no dial tone, try a phone wire from a phone that you know works. Get a dial tone now? If yes, the problem was with the original phone wire. Trash it and install a new one between the modem and the wall jack and try again.

If there's still no dial tone, try still another wall jack and another until you find one that works. If none of them work, you probably neglected to pay your phone bill.

Modem won't respond "OK" when you type AT commands

You or your software issue an AT command, but there's no answering message from the modem.

Probable cause: Either the cables are at fault or the software is set up incorrectly.

Solution: Make sure the cables are connected securely. Then check that the software is set for the correct port—that is, the port your modem is connected to. For example, if the modem is connected to COM2, the software will often default to COM1, so you have to find the software setting and change it.

Make sure, too, that you're typing in either uppercase or lowercase letters, not a combination. Be sure you press Enter at the end of a command.

Check the communications software manual to see if you're required to be in terminal mode to execute AT commands.

Check whether a fax is being sent or received. You can't use the data modem and the fax at the same time.

Problems Making a Connection

This section is all about what happens when the modem appears to be working fine, but you can't seem to make a connection.

Telephone rings but there's no answer

The connection appears to work normally, but the phone isn't answered at the other end.

Probable cause: Either you've dialed a wrong number or the packet network is overloaded.

Solution: Check to make sure you're dialing the right number. If you're dialing a packet-switching network to reach an on-line service, try again. If the problem persists, try another phone number in the network and leave a message on the service reporting the problem.

The system you called answers, but your modem makes no response

The phone is answered at the other end, but your modem just sits there doing nothing.

Probable cause: Cable connections are probably at fault—the modem may not have reset itself after some previous use.

Solution: Check your modem's cable connections. Use your communications software to send the command AT&F to your modem. This will reset it to its original settings. If this doesn't help, turn off your computer and modem and restart everything.

The system you're calling doesn't recognize your ID or password

You've enrolled in a bulletin board or other on-line system but when you call, the system treats you like a stranger.

Probable cause: The ID and password may be case-sensitive.

Solution: Try re-entering your password and ID in all uppercase or all lowercase letters. If this doesn't work, call the system's voice phone and ask for help.

Problems While You're Connected

The following section deals with difficulties that can arise after you've made a connection to another system.

The other system answers and you're connected, but lines of garbage characters scroll down your screen

You've enrolled in an on-line system but when you connect, you get only garbage on the screen.

Probable cause: You've signed on at a speed the other system can't handle. For example, you've specified 9600bps on a system that has a maximum speed of 2400bps.

Solution: Set your system to 2400bps and try again. 2400bps is likely to be recognized by almost any system.

File transfer fails before completion

You're tranferring one or more files, but the system fails in some mysterious way before the transfer is finished.

Probable cause: You may be using an incorrect protocol or flow control, or you may have a bad phone connection.

Solution: If you're using a mismatched protocol, the file transfer will fail immediately. Check that your protocol is exactly the same as the one being used at the other end. (*Kermit* is a common culprit in this, because there are so many versions of it out there.)

For a file transfer that fails part way through, you may not have configured your software for flow control. Consult your software's manual for information on *RTS/CTS* and *X-ON/X-OFF* and when to choose one or the other.

If you're using automated software (such as WinCIM, OzCIS, Prodigy, or America Online), file transfer will usually fail only when the line connection is bad.

Characters you type don't show on the screen, or they appear twice

When communicating online, your typing isn't echoed to the screen or it shows up double.

Probable cause: The duplex setting in the software is incorrect.

Solution: Change the duplex setting to the opposite of the current setting and try again.

Screen displays partially garbled text (parts of words are OK)

When you're communicating online, part of the screen display is muddled.

Probable cause: The parity setting is wrong.

Solution: If you're on at eight bits, change your parity setting to None. If you're on at seven bits, change the parity setting to Even or Odd—try the *opposite* of what you're using when the problem occurs.

Screen is garbled, displaying oddly spaced characters

The screen display is messed up, with some of the characters positioned peculiarly.

Probable cause: The data bit setting is wrong.

Solution: Change the software's data bit setting to seven or eight (the opposite of whatever it is when the problem occurs).

The bulletin board screen is a mixture of letters that make sense and letters that don't

You've connected to a bulletin board and some of the characters on the screen are nonsense.

Probable cause: You've signed on using VT100 terminal emulation to a bulletin board with a graphics interface.

Solution: Change the terminal emulation to ANSI BBS and try again.

You're typing commands to the remote system and nothing happens

In the middle of an on-line session, the remote system suddenly stops responding.

Probable cause: You've issued a Stop command, or the remote system may be having problems.

Solution: If you've accidentally entered the command Ctrl-S, this almost universal signal will cause the remote system to stop sending. Enter Ctrl-Q to restart things.

If this doesn't help, the remote system may be locked up. Enter Ctrl-C to see if that will bump you back to a menu of some sort. As a last resort, you may have to hang up and try again.

Call disconnects unexpectedly

Your phone connection drops even though you didn't issue a hang up command.

Probable cause: The connection is being interrupted.

Solution: If you have Call Waiting, make sure it's disabled. (You can disable Call Waiting by inserting *70,—*with* the comma—1170, if you have a dial phone, in front of the regular phone number.)

Check to see if anyone has picked up an extension phone, knocking you offline.

If you are interrupted repeatedly, it may be because of a noisy telephone line. Consult with the phone company; you may be able to get them to put a filter on your line.

Other Odds and Ends

Here are a couple of problems that don't fit into any of the other categories, but can drive you to distraction if you don't have the answers.

When someone sends you a fax, the fax modem won't answer

Someone tries to send you a fax and your fax modem refuses to accept it.

Probable cause: Auto-answer isn't set on the modem or in the software.

Solution: Check your software to see if there's an auto-answer setting. Set it to ON. If there's no such setting or if it's already set to ON, check your fax modem's manual to see if there's an auto-answer setting for the modem.

Modem's screeching noises make me crazy!

When you first start using a modem, the screeching noises emitted by the speakers can be strangely comforting. They let you know that something is indeed happening. But after a while, these noises can begin to sound like mating calls from an electronic zoo, and you may wish to be rid of them for good.

Probable cause: The modem's speaker is set to ON.

Solution: You can turn off the modem speaker by sending the command ATM0 (that's capital letters ATM and a *zero*) to your modem. All software has a place where the modem settings are kept. You may have to experiment with the placement in some cases.

On the other hand, if you just want to make the speaker quieter, the settings are:

ATL	Selects the lowest volume
ATL1	Selects low volume
ATL2	Selects medium volume (usually the factory default)
ATL3	Selects high volume

This way you can use your modem quietly without your significant other knowing that you're going online—again!

A Final Note

Most problems with modems are the result of being just a little too eager to jump in and get started. That might work with a word-processing program, but a modem requires just a bit more preparation.

Make sure you've installed the modem correctly. Read the modem manual and follow the instructions. If you get everything working and it suddenly stops, carefully think about what may have caused it. Installed new software? Changed some hardware? Get all your facts together before calling tech support.

If you can still connect to an on-line service, leave a detailed message there. If the modem doesn't work at all, call the voice technical support line. The vast majority of connect problems are very simple and can usually be resolved quickly.

Part Five

Troubleshooting

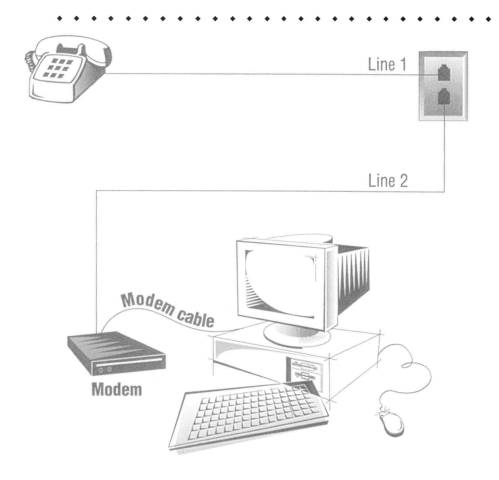

Line 1

Line 2

Modem cable

Modem

Sixteen

On-Line Tools and a Few Good Tips

· ·

Depending on the on-line services you use most, you'll soon develop your own list of tips and tricks that serve you well. Here are a few that have fairly wide application, along with the tools you'll need to put them in operation.

Get PKZIP and PKUNZIP

The software used most commonly by anyone online is PKZIP and PKUNZIP (pronounced pee-kay-ZIP and pee-kay-UNzip). PKZIP can take a file and compress it down to a fraction of its former size. PKUNZIP can decompress it back to its original size. This is a useful thing to be able to do for a variety of reasons. You may want to fit a large number of files on a single floppy, for example. More commonly, you will want to compress files before transmitting them by modem (to save on phone and on-line service charges). You'll also want to decompress them when you're at the receiving end.

The compression ratio for graphics files can be as much as 20 to 1. Graphics files have extensions like .BMP, .PCX, and .TIF. Word processing files are compressed down to about 40 percent of their uncompressed size. These files have extensions like .TXT or .DOC. The lowest ratio is for program files (.EXE), but even they can be reduced to half their original size. A file with the extension .ZIP has already been compressed and there's no advantage to doing it again.

 NOTE

Sometimes you'll get a compressed file or files with the extension .EXE. This is a self-extracting file—you run it just like a program and it decompresses the files it contains like magic!

Compression can save a lot of on-line time, particularly in the case of graphics files, but also text files. A 1MB graphic file can often be as small as 50Kb when compressed. This means that the uncompressed file will take 17–18 minutes to travel from one computer to another (using a 9600bps modem), while the compressed file will take less than a minute. When every minute online is costing money, this represents a substantial savings. The compression ratio for text files isn't so dramatic as for graphics files, but they're still shrunken by 50 to 70 percent.

Even if you're rolling in dough and don't care how long it takes to transfer a file, you'll still need PKZIP and PKUNZIP. This is because on-line services keep all their library and downloadable files in a zipped format. When you receive a file from an on-line service or bulletin board, it will usually have the file extension .ZIP, so you'll need to unzip it to see it. And if you belong to a service or bulletin board where you need to upload files, the system will almost certainly require you to zip up the file first.

Where to Find PKZIP and PKUNZIP

PKZIP and PKUNZIP are so commonly found on computers that many people believe them to be some sort of freeware. This isn't true. They're *shareware*, distributed by a company called PKWARE, Inc. If you use these programs, you are honor-bound to register and pay for them. This is a matter of honesty that is, alas, frequently disregarded. PKZIP and PKUNZIP are the most commonly pirated (that is, *stolen*) software products in the world.

There are two versions each of PKZIP and PKUNZIP. Just to confuse things, versions 1 and 2 don't recognize each other fully, so you'll need to download both. Most services are rapidly going over to version 2, but you'll still find files that have been compressed with version 1. The latest versions are in the self-extracting files PKZ110.EXE and PKZ204G.EXE. Put them in separate directories before decompressing. When they're uncompressed you'll have both PKZIP and PKUNZIP, as well as full documentation.

To find the files on CompuServe, GO PKWARE, which will take you to the PC Vendor C Forum. PKWARE maintains a library there (Library 11), where you'll find both versions.

America Online has both versions available but they are located in different spots. For version 1, select Go To Computing and Software, then click on the Software Center button, followed by the Helpful Utilities button. To find version 2, you also have to Go To Computing and Software, then double-click on Applications. From the Applications list, select Starter Kit. There you'll find PKZ204G.EXE ready for downloading.

Prodigy has PKZIP and PKUNZIP in the ZiffNet for Prodigy section. You have to pay to join ZiffNet ($7.50 per month for one hour's access time), so you're better off getting PKZIP from another source if you have one available.

Virtually all bulletin boards will have PKZIP and PKUNZIP files available for download, usually in the self-extracting form described above. Just poke around until you find them.

 NOTE

Files with the extension .ZIP have been compressed with PKZIP. Files with the extension .ARC have been compressed with an older archiving program that's increasingly rare, but still used. You'll need a program called ARC-E.EXE to decompress them. The ARC-E.EXE program can be found in the GO GRAPHICS Help section of CompuServe and in the ZiffNet section of Prodigy.

 **WARNING**

You may come across something called PKZ120.EXE on some bulletin boards. This purports to be the latest incarnation of version 1, but is in fact a crudely hacked revision of PZ110.EXE. PKWARE has disavowed this version and warns against its use.

 NOTE

The details of the on-line service CompuServe are covered in Chapter 8. There's lots more about America Online in Chapter 9, and Prodigy is chronicled in Chapter 7.

How to Use PKZIP and PKUNZIP

PKZIP and PKUNZIP are invaluable but not exactly intuitive. If you type either filename at a DOS prompt and press ↵, you'll get what purports to be help. Unfortunately, it's not helpful.

Fortunately, it's not all that difficult to get the basic operation straight. For unzipping a zipped file, the format is as follows: type, **PKUNZIP**, followed by the name of the file you want to decompress, followed by where you want the unzipped file to go. (In all cases, the current directory is assumed unless you specify another.)

So, if you've downloaded a file called PSP.ZIP into a directory called C:\MODEM and you'd like the unzipped file or files to end up in a directory called C:\GRAPHICS, type the following:

        PKUNZIP C:\MODEM\PS.ZIP C:\GRAPHICS

To compress a file, reverse the process. The syntax then is: PKZIP, followed by the name of the new zipped file you want to create, followed by the name of the file you want to zip up.

If you want to zip up a letter in your WINWORD directory, type:

        PKZIP LETTER.ZIP C:\WINWORD\LETTER.DOC

The new file would be called LETTER.ZIP and it would be in your root directory (unless you specified a path to another location). You can do lots of fancy things with PKZIP and PKUNZIP, but for that you'll have to read the documentation (don't forget to register!).

Get a GIF Viewer and Converter

 NOTE

For more on Compuserve and its workings, see Chapter 8.

Most graphics images stored on on-line services (and all of the really good ones) are in a format pioneered by CompuServe called Graphics Interchange Format (GIF). GIF files can be viewed, printed, and converted into other formats, but in order to do that, you'll need a GIF viewer and/or converter.

Because of CompuServe's role in setting the GIF standard, it has the largest supply of GIF viewing and converting programs. However, most of these programs and many others can be found on other services as well.

If you're using WinCIM, you don't need a separate program to view GIF files. Go to the graphics forums (GO GRAPHICS) and select what you want from the various graphics collections. Figure 16.1 shows a list of GIF images available in a sublibrary called Animal Kingdom under the larger heading of Quick Pictures. You can highlight a file and click on Description for more information.

TIP

To download several pictures at a time, put an × in the box next to the ones you want, then click the Retrieve button.

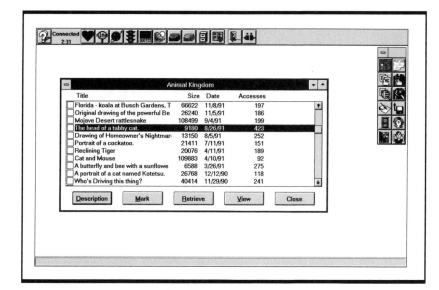

Figure 16.1

One of many, many lists of graphics files available from CompuServe

If you click on the View button, the actual picture will be displayed on screen, as shown in Figure 16.2. Once the picture is displayed, you can save it to your hard disk by selecting Save!

Figure 16.2
A GIF file displayed in WinCIM

For other GIF viewers on CompuServe, GO GRAPHSUP to reach the Graphics Support Forum and then Search the GIF Viewers section of the library. For America Online, Go To Computing and Software. There, you can click on Graphics and Animation.

Among the best GIF viewers and converters available are:

Filename, Program	What It Does	Where to Get It
PSP.ZIP Paint Shop Pro	Lets you view, convert, print, and manipulate GIF, BMP, TIF, PCX, and a dozen other formats—this one does everything	CompuServe, America Online, Prodigy
WINGIF.ZIP Wingif	Lets you view and convert GIF, PCX, and BMP files	CompuServe, America Online, ZiffNet for Prodigy
VUIMAGE.EXE View Image	Lets you view and print GIF and many other file formats	CompuServe, America Online
TAGVUE.EXE TagVue	Provides a viewer for "first time users"	CompuServe, America Online

Filename, Program	What It Does	Where to Get It
CSHOWA.EXE CompuShow	Provides a full-featured DOS viewer of many graphics file formats (this is an oldie but definitely a goodie)	CompuServe, America Online
WGIF.ZIP SWGIF1.1A	Gives you a Windows 3.1 GIF viewer that's quick to download	Compuserve

GIF viewers and converters are available from every bulletin board or commercial service that features GIF files online. All of them are at least shareware (and sometimes even *free*ware, for which you pay nothing), so you have little to lose by trying a number of them until you find one or more that you like. Remember—you're under no obligation to register and pay for shareware if you try it and decide you don't want to use it. All of the programs listed above are shareware, except WGIF.ZIP, which is freeware.

Pick Your Phone Numbers Carefully

Because the clock is running every time you get online, it behooves you to do whatever research is necessary to make sure you're doing it as economically as possible. Take into consideration the following:

- If the service charges more for higher bps access, think about what you're going to be doing online. Just pottering? Sign on at the cheapest rate. Downloading files? Sign on at the fastest rate.
- What if the fastest rate is only available at a number that's a toll-call away? No escape here, you'll have to do the math and find out if the toll charges offset the gain you get from using a faster modem speed.
- Consider that a call to a neighboring state may actually be less-per-minute than an intra-state call. Particularly in the northeastern U.S., it may be cheaper for you to call over a state line than to call within your own state. Check the rates.

- Find out if the system you want to access lets you call through a packet-switching network. Using a packet-switching network can cost $2–$6 an hour, but if it saves you $10 an hour in long distance charges, it's still a bargain. See "A Few Words about Telephone Networks" in Chapter 7 for more on this mode of communication.

Automate Your Access Whenever Possible

Because the on-line services make money only while you're actually on-line, it's in their interest to keep you signed on for as long as possible. And it's your mission, of course, to outwit them to the extent that you can. Here are some tips for using the major systems economically.

CompuServe

NOTE
Chapter 8 has more general information on CompuServe.

As soon as you know your way around the system, download OzCIS (GO OZCIS) and set it up to fetch your mail and forum messages. OzCIS takes a bit of effort to get going, but by using it you can cut your on-line time by 75 percent or more.

Read and compose all your mail offline. Sign on only to make the exchange. If you're browsing, sign on at 2400bps; if you're downloading files or messages, sign on at the fastest modem speed available.

Prodigy

NOTE
The details of Prodigy use are covered in Chapter 7.

Buy the Royston Utilities (JUMP ROYSTON) and use them to read and write all your messages offline. Set the Working icon to become a timer so you can keep track of the amount of time you spend online.

Use the Copy command to print out screens of text so you can read them later. For even more time savings, use Copy Options from the Tools menu to send screens to a file on your hard disk and read them later.

America Online

Use the Logging feature to avoid spending time reading material on-line. Before you start a session, select Logging from the File menu and open a session log. All the text you encounter will be saved into a file you can read later by selecting File▶Open and highlighting the SESSION.LOG. If you forget to start a session log and later come across a document you want to read offline, select File▶Save. All the text in the article in the frontmost window will be saved to a file and location you specify. You don't have to display the entire article for it to be saved. All of it is copied to a file when you issue the Save command.

Another way to minimize your on-line time is to compose all your mail offline, then sign on to send it. You should also keep track of your money by regularly checking your current bill (keyword: Billing).

NOTE
The nuts-and-bolts about America Online is covered in Chapter 9.

Other Services

To save money on other services, pay attention to the rules you may have paid little attention to when you first signed up. For example, some services have drastically different rates for use, depending on the time of day. The SprintNet and Tymnet networks that most people use to access DELPHI, for example, charge $9 per hour during business hours; but there's no network charge at all for access from 7PM to 6AM on weekdays or anytime Saturday and Sunday.

Also, when you're paying by the minute, you'll save money if you sign on at times when the system is less busy. Your time on the system is allocated in slices. These time-slices get smaller as the system becomes busier. That means your computer spends more time waiting in line for data, and less time actually transmitting and receiving.

Almost all systems are busier in the evenings. Systems utilized a lot by individuals for recreation and entertainment are busier on the weekends. When you have files to download or many messages to retrieve, take advantage of knowing this by scheduling your session for early in the morning (eastern U.S.) or late in the evening (western U.S.).

NOTE
You'll find more about DELPHI in Chapter 10.

A Final Note

All the major on-line services and most of the smaller ones will give you some kind of deal in your first month of membership. CompuServe, America Online, and Prodigy all give you your first month's membership free and throw in some free on-line time.

This is the time you want to spend getting to know the system. In many cases, the free time doesn't carry over to the next month, so use it all as soon as you can. For example, DELPHI offers five free hours during the month you join. If you join on the last day of the month, your five free hours have to be used that day or they're gone!

For this reason, you shouldn't join a whole raft of on-line services all at once—no matter how great the temptation. Join one service, get familiar with it, and use up whatever freebies you get. Once you feel comfortable with that service, think about joining another, but don't rush into it. It's very easy to find yourself running up big bills without meaning to.

On the other hand, the rewards of being online can be enormous. You have access to information you couldn't get easily any other way. You can stay on top of subjects that interest you and *develop* an interest in others. You can make new friends and stay in contact with old friends far away.

It's a big world and your computer and modem can put you in touch with just about any part of it. A wonderful adventure awaits you there.

The Hayes AT
Command Set

• •

To use your modem, you need modem communications software, such as ProComm or Crosstalk or Microlink. With this software, you can mostly use your modem without knowing anything at all about AT commands, because the software hides the gruesome details from you. However, the time may come when you want to make changes to the commands in say, your America Online software. Or you may just want to be able to decipher the commands being issued.

Many, many commands make up the entire set of modem control commands known as the Hayes AT Command Set. Your modem will support only some subset of the commands, so you'll need to check the modem manual for all the AT commands supported by your modem.

In this appendix you'll find descriptions of the most prevalent commands and how they're used.

AT Attention

Every modem command (except the A/ command and the escape sequence[+++]) must begin with the characters *AT*. *AT* stands for *AT*tention and may precede a single command or a series of commands. The **AT** command must be all uppercase or all lowercase. The modem will not understand *aT* or *At* to be an attention command.

A modem command line has the syntax:

AT *commands*

AT is the attention code that must begin every line. The *commands* are one or more of the AT Command Set. To end the line you must press the ↵ key. You can include spaces in the command line to improve readability, as I've done in all the examples in this appendix. Unfortunately, most of the time in manuals and books less friendly than this one, the codes are shown all run together like this:

ATS0=0Q0v1X4&c1\JO\N0

etc., etc., so you have to pry the commands apart piece by piece to see what's going on.

A/ Repeat the last command line

Repeat last command. Used when a line is busy or doesn't answer, for example. This command doesn't begin with the AT prefix nor does it require a ↵ at the end.

Command Mode and On-Line Mode

The modem is always in either *command* mode or *on-line* mode. The modem starts up in command mode. In this mode all data you send to the modem is interpreted as modem commands. Once you've made a connection to a remote computer, the modem switches to on-line mode. In this mode, the modem interprets all information it receives as data.

+++ This is the default escape sequence. When the modem detects these characters it returns to command mode from the on-line mode. Does not require AT before the command or a ↵ key after the command.

O Command to return to on-line mode from command mode.

A Manual answer

Command to answer incoming call immediately.

D Dial phone number

Dial command. The command ATD*n* is used to dial a telephone number (*n* represents the telephone number). Spaces, hyphens, and parentheses can be used for clarity; the modem ignores them. Tone dialing is the default. A number of modifiers can be used with the **D** command:

T and P   T and P specify *t*one or *p*ulse dialing.

W   W causes the modem to *w*ait for a subsequent dial tone. For example, the following command dials 9 for an outside line and then waits for a dial-tone before continuing to dial:

    AT D 9 W 212-555-2525

Comma (,)   The comma (,) modifier causes a pause of two seconds while dialing. It's often used when dialing call waiting to allow time for the return of the dial tone. The following command does just that:

    AT D *70,1 415 555 1212

Semicolon (;)   The semicolon (;) modifier returns the modem to command mode after dialing the number without connecting to the remote modem. This is useful if you need to dial a sequence of numbers longer than the 40-character command-line limit (such as for banking by phone). For example, the following commands dial a single phone number, but the connection to remote modem is not made until after the second line:

> AT DT 9,1-916-555-1212;
> AT DT 455-56733-844#

! Using the ! modifer is equivalent to depressing the switch hook for $\frac{1}{2}$ second.

@ The @ modifier causes the modem to wait for quiet. Some telephone systems don't offer a dial tone when accessed; this command tells the modem to wait for five seconds of silence before performing the next command.

S The S modifier indicates a stored number. The command to dial a stored number is

> ATDS=n

where n is the location of the number you stored with the **&Z** command.

DL Redial

The command **AT DL** will redial the last telephone number. This command is similar to **A/** except that it does require the prefix **AT** and it simply redials the number without sending the entire command line again as **A/** does.

H Hang up

This command hangs up the phone:

> AT H

L Speaker volume

The command **L** controls the speaker volume:

L	Very low volume
L1	Low volume
L2	Medium volume
L3	High volume

M Speaker on or off

The **M** command turns the speaker on and off:

M	Speaker always off
M1	Speaker on until carrier detected
M2	Speaker always on
M3	Speaker off when carrier is detected and during dialing

^M Carriage return

^M Represents a carriage return (↵) when placed at the end of a command line.

Q Enable or disable result codes

The **Q** command enables or disables the modem's ability to show result codes such as CONNECT, BUSY, RING, and so forth, on your computer screen. Q1 prevents the display of result codes. Q0 causes the result codes to be displayed. Q0 is the default setting.

&F Restore factory profile

The **&F** (*at factory*) command restores the original modem settings.

&V View profiles

&V allows you to view configuration profiles (stored with **&W**) and telephone numbers (stored with **&Z**).

&W Write configuration profile

Place **&W** at the end of any command line and any option changed in that line will be permanently saved (*written*).

&Z Store telephone number

Stores a phone number in the modem's memory. The syntax is:

    AT &Zn=number

233

where *n* is a location where the number will be stored. Some modems can store only one number, so it would always be in location 0 (zero). Others can store up to ten, so they can be in locations 0 through 9. *Number* is the phone number and its dial modifiers. This command stores a phone number:

    AT &Z0=*70,1-516-555-1212

and this command will dial the number just stored:

    AT DS=0

The number will be retained in memory even when the modem is turned off.

\T Inactivity timer

The command \T tells the modem to disconnect if no activity has occurred in the time specified. The syntax is:

    AT \T*n*

where *n* specifies the number of minutes to wait.

%C Enable or disable MNP data compression

Using the command %C specifies whether MNP-5 data compression is used. Some on-line services may ask you to disable MNP-5 for more reliable transmissions. The syntax is:

    AT %C*n*

When *n* is 0, MNP-5 data compression is *disabled*. When *n* is 1, MNP-5 is *enabled*.

S Registers

Hayes-compatible modems maintain their settings in memory locations called *S registers*. The registers are numbered S0, S1, S2, and so forth. The total number of S registers will vary depending on your modem, but most modems have thirty or more.

The contents of some S registers are:

S0   Indicates whether the modem will answer a call. Setting S0 to 0 disables auto-answer. Any other number will specify the number of times the phone can ring before the modem answers.

S1	Counts the number of rings (in auto-answer mode).
S2	Holds the ASCII value of the escape sequence character. The factory setting is 43, the ASCII value of the + sign.
S3	Holds the ASCII value of the carriage return character. The factory setting is 13.
S6	Indicates number of seconds to wait before dialing. The purpose of the delay is to wait for a dial tone. The factory setting is usually 2 seconds.
S7	Indicates number of seconds to wait for a connection. If the setting for this register is 30 seconds, the modem will allow that much time for the call to be completed. Then the timer will be reset for another 30 seconds for the handshake to be completed.
S8	Indicates number of seconds to pause for each comma. When you include the comma modifier in a phone number the modem pauses for the length of time specified in this register. The default is usually 2 seconds.

Reading an S Register   To read the contents of an S register, use the following command:

    AT S*n*?

where *n* represents the number of the S register you want to read. In response, the modem displays a three-digit number indicating the contents of the requested register. It also displays "OK" on the next line. For example, this command reads the contents of register S3:

    ATS3?

The modem responds with:

    013
    OK

Writing an S Register   To write a value to an S register, use the following command:

    AT S*n=value*

235

where *n* is the number of the S register you want to write to and *value* is the value you want to set the register to. For example, this command sets the S0 register to 3:

AT S0=3

The modem responds with:

OK

If the command you need isn't in this listing, you'll have to consult the documentation that came with your modem. The manual should list all the commands that your modem knows how to use.

Appendix B

Popular On-Line Services

● ●

The danger of presenting a list of on-line services is that changes occur regularly. It's possible that a phone number may change or (more likely) that the maximum modem speed will increase on many of these services. If you're interested, call and ask. All these companies are delighted to answer questions and send you promotional material describing why they're the best.

237

Service	Specialty	Maximum Modem Speed (bps)	Voice Phone
America Online	Everything	9600	800-827-6364
AT&TMail	E-mail	2400	800-624-5672
BRS	General databases	9600	800-955-0906
BIX	PC and technical information	9600	800-695-4775
CompuServe	Everything	14400	800-848-8199
DASNet	E-mail	9600	408-559-7434
DataTimes	Financial services, newspapers, magazines	9600	800-642-2525
DELPHI	Everything	9600	800-695-4005
DIALOG	Business, science, news	9600	800-334-2564
Dow Jones Information Services	Financial news	9600	800-522-3567
EasyNet	General databases	9600	800-220-9553
GEnie	Everything	9600	800-638-9636
Mead Data Central LEXIS\NEXIS	News and legal information	9600	800-227-4908
MEDLARS	Medical information	9600	800-638-8480
MCI Mail	E-mail	9600	800-444-6245
National Videotex Network	Everything	9600	800-336-9096
NewsNet	Newsletters	9600	800-952-0122

Table B.2

What should be on the box (or in the ad) when you are buying a 14,400bps modem

Service	Specialty	Maximum Modem Speed (bps)	Voice Phone
ORBIT	Trademark and patent services	9600	800-955-0906
Prodigy	Everything	9600	800-776-3449
SprintMail	E-mail	9600	800-736-1130
The Well	Everything	9600	415-332-4335
WESTLAW	Legal information	9600	800-937-8529
Ziffnet	PC and technical information	14400	800-635-6225

Appendix C

Resource Guide

• • • • • • • • • • • • • • • • • • • •

This appendix contains names, addresses, and phone numbers for suppliers of products and services mentioned in this book.

NOTE

For the phone numbers of on-line services, see Appendix B. A list of Internet access providers is included in Chapter 10.

Calera Recognition Systems
475 Potrero Avenue
Sunnyvale, CA 94086
408-720-8300
WordScan Plus OCR software

Datastorm Technologies
PO Box 1471
Columbia, MO 65205
314-443-3282
ProComm Plus, ProComm Plus for Windows

DCA
1000 Alderman Drive
Alpharetta, GA 30202
800-348-3221
Crosstalk Communicator, Crosstalk for Windows

Delrina Corporation
6830 Via Del Oro
Suite 240
San Jose, CA 95119-1353
800-268-6082
WinFax Pro

DigiBoard
6400 Flying Cloud Drive
Eden Prairie, MN 55344
800-344-4273
DigiBoard 2Port

FutureSoft Engineering
12012 Wickchester Lane, Suite 600
Houston, TX 77079
713-496-9400
DynaComm

Hayes Microcomputer Products
PO Box 105203
Atlanta, GA 30348
404-441-1617
modems, Smartcom

Intel Corporation
5200 N.E. Elam Young Parkway
Hillsboro, OR 97124
503-629-7000
SatisFAXtion modems, Faxability Plus software

Microcom Inc.
500 River Ridge Drive
Norwood, MA 02062
800-822-8224
Carbon Copy Plus, Carbon Copy for Windows

Micro Warehouse
1720 Oak Street
Lakewood, NJ 08701
800-367-7080
mail order software and hardware

Micro Werks
PO Box 768273
Roswell, GA 30076
BBS: 404-410-9358
CIS: 72510,1766
Microlink

Multi-Link, Inc.
225 Industry Parkway
Nicholasville, KY 40356
606-885-6363
The Stick

MultiTech Systems
2205 Woodale Drive
Mounds View, MN 55112
800-328-9717
modems

National Semiconductor
PO Box 58090
Santa Clara, CA 95052-8090
408-721-5000
TyIN 2000, TyIN 4000

Ozarks West Software
14150 Gleneagle Drive
Colorado Springs, CO 80921
CIS: 70007,3574
OzCIS

PC Connection
6 Mill Street
Marlow, NH 03456
800-800-5555
mail order software and hardware

Phoenix Technologies
Three First National Plaza
Suite 1616
Chicago, IL 60602
800-452-0120
Eclipse FAX

PKWare, Inc.
9025 N. Deerwood Drive
Brown Deer, WI 53223
414-354-8699
PKZIP, PKUNZIP

Practical Peripherals
375 Conejo Ridge Avenue
Thousand Oaks, CA 91361
805-497-4774
modems

Prometheus Products Inc.
9524 S.W. Tualatin Sherwood Road
Tualatin, OR 97062
503-692-9600
Ultima Home Office

Royston Development
4195 Chino Hills Parkway #510
Chino Hills, CA 91709
JUMP: ROYSTON
PRO-UTIL software for Prodigy

SoftKlone Distributing Corp.
327 Office Plaza Drive
Tallahassee, FL 32301
800-634-8670
Mirror

Support Group, Inc.
Lake Technology Park
McHenry, MD 21541
800-872-4768
TapCIS

Symantec Corporation
10201 Torre Avenue
Cupertino, CA 95014
800-441-7234
pcANYWHERE, Norton Utilities

Telcor Systems Corporation
4 Strathmore Road
Natick, MA 01760
508-653-3995
T/Port, T/PorTwin

WordPerfect Corporation
1555 N. Technology Way
Orem, UT 84057
801-222-5800
WordPerfect 6 for DOS

Zoom Telephonics
207 South Street
Boston, MA 02111
800-631-3116
modems

Glossary

Glossary

* *

In general, the worst thing about modems and computer communications is the bizarre technical language and jargon that modem geeks use. I've tried to avoid the weirder stuff in this book (or at least define it as we went along), but I can't protect you forever. So here are definitions of terms you're likely to stumble across as you venture forth.

247

8250 UART   The UART used for the communications ports on most older computers. (*See also* UART.)

16450 UART   The UART used on some 80286 computers. (*See also* UART.)

16550 UART   The UART used with most newer computers and high-speed modems. Variations include the 16550A, 16550AF, and 16550AFN. All include a buffer so that the UART can hold some data when data is sent or received faster than the computer or modem can handle. (*See also* UART.)

Acoustic Modem   A modem that connects to a telephone via rubber caps placed over the telephone handset. Originally developed to get around telephone company regulations that prohibited connecting directly to telephone lines. These regulations are now defunct, and so are acoustic modems for the most part.

Analog signal   The signal a modem uses to communicate with another modem.

ANSI   (Pronounced AN-see.) Acronym for the *American National Standards Institute*. An organization that sets standards including one for codes that control cursor movement, colors, and other display attributes.

Archive   To compress files with PKZIP, LHARC, or some other program. Such compressed files will have the extension .ZIP, .ARC, or .LZH. The programs used to archive and unarchive files are found on most on-line services.

ASCII   (Pronounced ASK-ee.) Stands for the *American Standard Code for Information Interchange*. It uses 7 bits to represent letters of the alphabet as well as numbers, punctuation marks, and other characters. ASCII often uses 8 bits in the form of bytes and ignores the first bit.

Auto-Answer   When a modem can automatically pick up the phone and attempt to connect with a calling modem.

Background Send/Receive   The ability of a fax modem to send or receive faxes while the computer is being used for other purposes.

Baud   The speed at which data is transmitted over a communications line. This is being replaced by *bits per second* (bps) as a more accurate unit of measurement.

BBS   Bulletin board system. A small on-line service usually operated by only one person, a manufacturer (to provide product support), or a special interest group.

Bit   A *Binary digIT*. Represents a single switch inside a computer set to 0 (zero) or 1. Eight bits make up a byte, the basic unit of data storage.

Bits per second   Unit of measurement for data transmission. Abbreviated *bps*.

Block   A group of data bytes. For example, when transferring a file, blocks of 128 or of 1024 characters are often sent.

Byte   A group of 8 bits. Roughly equivalent to one character.

Buffer   A place in memory where data is stored temporarily until the computer or modem is ready for it. Buffers enable faster transfer rates.

Capture   To catch text that is being sent to your computer from a BBS and put it in a buffer or a file. Most communications programs have capture options so you can read material offline.

Carrier Signal   The tone sent by the modem before any data. The frequency is modified to indicate data.

CAS   *Communications Application Specification*. A standard from Intel defining methods of sending and receiving of fax information to and from Group III fax machines.

CCITT   The *Comité Consultatif International de Télégraphique et Téléphonique*. Established by the United Nations, this group sets world-wide communications standards. Most of their recommendations having to do with modems and faxes are in the V series (V.21, V.32, V.32*bis*, and so forth).

Characters per second (Abbreviated *cps.*) The number of bytes or characters that can be sent over a phone line in one second. This is determined by dividing the bps rate by the number of bits it takes to send one byte (usually 10—the start bit, 8 bits of data, and the stop bit). So, a 9600bps modem can theoretically send 960cps.

Checksum A number that represents a larger group of numbers in order to check for errors in data transmission. It is commonly used when downloading a program, as well as in error-checking protocols. The checksum is the result of a mathematical equation.

COM port A *COM*munications connection point on your computer used for a serial device such as a modem. Most PCs have COM1 and COM2; some will also have COM3 and COM4. An external modem plugs into an available COM port. An internal modem *becomes* a COM port (at least as far as the software is concerned).

Connect speed The speed your modem uses when it connects with a BBS. This speed will depend on the speed of your modem, and the BBS's modem. It will be no higher than the lower of the two speeds. If you have a 9600bps modem, and call a 2400bps BBS, your connect speed will be 2400bps.

Control character Any of the 32 ASCII characters that don't print on your screen or printer. These characters are the first 32 in the list of ASCII characters and are used to control your computer.

CRC Stands for *Cyclical Redundancy Checking.* CRC is a system to make sure that a block of data (usually from a downloaded file) is free from error. It's usually 16 or 32 bits long.

Data compression Some modems can *compress* data so that it takes up less space. When another modem (that also has this capability) receives the data, it expands the data to its original form. By using data compression, a modem can send information faster. It's a lot like shorthand—the information is still there, but it takes less space and is quicker. MNP and V.42*bis* are current methods of data compression.

Default   The setting that the device or program will have without any intervention from you.

DIP switches   Stands for *Dual Inline Package*, tiny switches mounted on electronic equipment. Most internal modems and a few external modems have them. Used to change the default settings.

Download   To receive a computer file from another modem.

Duplex   The ability of both sides of a connection to send information at the same time. *Full-duplex* is the same as duplex.

EIA-232-D   (*Also called* RS-232 and RS-232D.) This is the standard for communications between a PC and a modem. The interface consists of 25 wires, although a variation contains 9 wires. Modem cables are known as EIA-232-D cables or RS-232 cables.

E-mail   (*Also called* Electronic mail.) Messages that are sent electronically to individual people. You choose who to send the message to and only that person receives the message.

Emoticons   (*Also called* smileys.) Groups of characters that are used to express emotion in written communication. For example, :-) is a happy face (when you look at it from the side). Similarly, :-(is a sad face. (*See* the inside front cover for a listing.)

External modem   A modem that's located outside the computer. It's hooked up to the computer with a cable, most commonly an EIA-232-D cable.

Factory configuration   The way your modem came, set up from the factory. Send the command **ATZ** to your modem to return it to the factory configuration.

Fall-back   The ability of a modem to change to a lower speed when there's a problem communicating at its normal, higher speed. Often necessary to make a reliable connection over noisy phone lines.

Forum   An area within an on-line service where messages are exchanged on specific topics. Forums often include a library area where programs are stored for downloading.

Freeware   Computer programs that are copyrighted but may be legally copied for noncommercial purposes. Almost the same as public domain programs, except that public domain programs are not copyrighted and may be sold.

Gateway   A connection between one network and another. For example, on some commercial on-line services you can buy airline tickets. This usually involves the on-line service you called connecting you to the airline's computer.

Group I Fax   Obsolete international fax standard that supported transmission at the rate of six-minutes per page. Not supported by today's fax modems or fax machines.

Group II Fax   Second international fax standard supporting transmission at the rate of three-minutes per page. Still supported by Group III machines.

Group III Fax   The current international fax standard supporting transmission rates of one-minute (or less) per page. All fax boards and machines sold today should support Group III.

Group IV Fax   A recent international fax standard supporting transmission rates up to 19.2Kbps. This standard is defined for digital telephones and is not used in public systems at this time.

Half-duplex   A mode which allows only one modem at a time to transmit information. When one modem is finished, the other can then start to transmit.

Hand-shaking   The process of establishing an electronic link between two modems. Handshaking establishes information such as the speed and error-correction method they'll be using.

Hayes-compatible   Any modem which operates in the same way as the modems developed by Hayes. Any modem sold for general use should be Hayes-compatible.

Host   A computer being used to store information from other computers. Every BBS and on-line service is a host.

Initialize   To prepare hardware or software for use. Many modems have to be initialized each time they're used so they know how to act with the communications program.

Internal modem   A modem on a printed circuit board (*card*) that occupies one of the slots in a PC. It's connected directly to the phone outlet by a standard phone wire.

Interrupt   An interrupt is an urgent request for the central processor's attention. Devices (such as modems) that perform input/output functions can issue an interrupt to stop the currently running program so the CPU can service the request. The same interrupt cannot be used by two devices running at the same time.

Kermit   A file transfer protocol developed at Columbia University. It's very adaptable and transfers in blocks of varying size. Somewhat finicky in use, however.

LAPM   *Link Access Procedure for Modems*. A type of error control included in the V.42 protocol. It's *not* a compression method, although some modem manufacturers incorrectly advertise it as such.

Line noise   This is interference on telephone lines. Can cause one character or many characters of garbage to appear on your screen. In general, the higher the bps rate of your modem, the more vulnerable it is to line noise. Error-checking protocols can get rid of most noise.

Logoff   To leave an on-line connection. When you choose to logoff, the BBS will usually ask if that's what you really want to do, then it will disconnect.

Logon   The process of connecting to a BBS or other on-line service. *Also:* What occurs after the other computer has answered the phone but before you actually start using the service. Logon can include the process of entering your name and password (which is also called *sign-on*).

MNP   Microcom Networking Protocol. A type of error control and data compression, created by Microcom. It's built into the modem, unlike software error correction in file transfer protocols. Levels 1–4 are error control protocols, and Level 5 specifies two types of data compression. A modem with MNP-5 also has MNP-4. MNP 1–4 is included in the CCITT V.42 error correction standards.

Mode   The state a computer or a program is in. For example, a computer can be in a *text mode* or *graphics mode*. A communications program can also be in a *chat mode* (which operates differently than the normal mode).

Modem   A contraction of *MODulator/DEModulator*. A device that allows computers to communicate over telephone lines.

Modular connector   The plug at the end of a phone cord or the socket into which it's inserted. In the U.S. and Canada, RJ-11 connectors are used between the telephone base unit and the wall socket. *Also:* The cable connecting a modem to the wall socket also uses RJ-11 connectors. RJ-22 connectors are used between the telephone handset and the base unit.

Online   When your computer is actively connected to another computer over telephone lines.

Packet-switching network   A data network that relays computer data from one area to another. The networks allow you to use a local telephone number to access thousands of public and private on-line services. The two major packet-switching networks in the United States are SprintNet and Tymnet.

Parity bit   An extra bit that may be added to any character that has 7 or fewer data bits to aid in error detection. The setting can be no parity, mark parity, space parity, odd parity, or even parity.

Pocket modem An *external modem* that is small enough to be easily portable. It uses a battery for power, or gets its power from the phone line.

Protocol A set of rules that determine the flow of data and how it's used. The modems at either end of a communications link have to be using the same protocol to talk to each other. *Same as:* error-checking protocol. There are protocols for file transfers (XMODEM, YMODEM, ZMODEM, Kermit), for error correction (MNP, V.42), and for data compression (MNP-5 and V.42*bis*).

Public domain A program or file in the public domain usually has no copyright, can be copied legally by anybody, and has no restrictions on its use.

RJ-11 A normal phone connector. Modems usually have two jacks of this type: one to connect to the phone line, and the other to connect to a telephone. (*See also* modular connector.)

RS-232 *See* EIA-232-D.

Script language A programming language that is provided with a communications program, this enables you to write *scripts* to automate certain functions on your computer, such as making unattended calls to bulletin boards to do late-night downloads.

Settings Information that describes the way your computer and another computer should be connected. The first digit is normally 7 or 8, the number of data bits. The second character is a letter describing the parity (N for None, M for Mark, S for Space, O for Odd, and E for Even). The last number is the number of stop bits. **8N1** is the most common setting.

Shareware Programs that can be distributed freely and tried without obligation. If you like it, you are honor-bound to register and pay the usually modest fee.

SIG Special Interest Group. This is similar to a message base, but it may also contain files. Used on larger systems to designate areas of interest. Similar to a *forum*.

Sysop   Short for *SYStems OPerator*. This is the person who is in charge of a BBS or a forum. On a large commercial service, serves as mentor, guide, and traffic cop. On smaller services, the sysop is the final authority on everything.

Throughput   The rate of *useful* data bits sent after data compression has been accounted for. For example, a modem rated at 9600bps can, theoretically, through the use of V. 42 data compression, achieve a throughput of 38.4Kbps. No more than 9600bps are being transmitted but they represent 38.4K bits of real information after they are decoded.

UART   Universal *Asynchronous Receiver/Transmitter*. A chip on your motherboard or serial interface card that changes serial data (the way data comes in over the phone line) to parallel, and vice versa. This chip performs a variety of tasks and can easily become a bottleneck on faster systems. In systems running Windows with high-speed processors (386-33 or better), the newer 16550 UART may be the only way to get high-speed communications to work properly.

Unarchive   To decompress files that have been compressed with a program such as PKZIP or LHARC. (*See also* Archive.)

Upload   Transferring a file from your computer to another.

V.14   A data-conversion standard incorporated in all V.32 and V.32*bis* modems.

V.17   The CCITT standard for fax transmission at 14,400bps (14.4Kbps).

V.21   CCITT standard that controls transmission at 300bps. Same as Bell 103.

V.22   The international standard for transmission at 1200bps, created by CCITT. Same as Bell 212A.

V.22bis   CCITT standard for data transmission at 2400bps.

V.32 International standard controlling transmission at 9600bps, created by CCITT. V.32 has provisions for fallback to 4800bps if the line is too noisy.

V.32bis International standard for modems operating at 14.4Kbps with fallback rates of 12Kbps and 7.2Kbps, including the rates supported by V.32.

V.32terbo A nonofficial standard specifying modems operating at 19.2Kbps with fallback rates of 16.2Kbps and the rates supported by V.32 and V.32*bis*. The misspelling of "turbo" is deliberate. It's a play on the proper CCITT suffix for the third iteration of a standard, which would be *ter*.

V.34 Scheduled to be approved in mid-1994, this will be the CCITT standard for modems operating at 28.8Kbps.

V.42 A standard error-control system for modems. It includes LAPM, as well as MNP 2–4.

V.42bis A CCITT standard for data compression. Any modem with V.42*bis* also includes V.42 error control.

V.FAST The informal designation for modems up to 28.8Kbps, manufactured before the CCITT approval of the V.34 specifications.

X.400 This is the CCITT standard protocol for a global system for the exchange of electronic mail (e-mail).

X.500 The CCITT standard for a directory of the users of the X.400 system.

XMODEM A file transfer protocol developed by Ward Christensen in the late 1970s. It's quite slow by today's standards, but was the first widespread file transfer protocol. Xmodem uses blocks of 128 bytes, and after each block is sent, it sends a 1 byte checksum to check for errors. If an error is encountered, the block is sent again. Almost every communications program offers this protocol.

XMODEM/CRC The same as XMODEM with the addition of a 16-bit CRC instead of the checksum, which makes it more reliable.

YMODEM   Similar to XMODEM/CRC, except it uses blocks of 1024 bytes, rather than 128. This makes it faster than XMODEM, since it needs to stop less often to check for errors. Sometimes called XMODEM-1K.

ZMODEM   A file transfer protocol known for its speed, as well as its ability to transfer information about the files being sent. It has crash recovery and auto-download features, and can use a 32-bit CRC, which makes it almost error free. The file-transfer protocol of choice under most circumstances.

Index

••••••••••••••••••••••••••••••••

Page numbers in **bold** refer to primary explanations of topics. Page numbers in *italic* refer to illustrations.

A

ANSI-BBS terminal emulation, 59, 158, 214
answering calls
  auto-answer, 215, 248
  modem command for, 231
  problems in, **211**, 215
ARC-E.EXE program, 221
.ARC files, 221
Archie utility, **148**
archive files, 132, 220, 248
ARPA (Advanced Research Projects Agency), 135
ARPAnet, 135
ASCII (American Standard Code of Information Interchange), 248
ASCII files, **164**
ASSIST program (Prodigy), 94
asynchronous modems, 6
AT commands, 63, **210**, **229–236**
at signs (@) as modem command, 232
AT&TMail, **178**
Attach File dialog box (America Online), 168, *168*
·auto-answering, 215, 248
Auto-Filed folder on CompuServe, 108
AUTOLOGON tool (Prodigy), **86**
automatic callback in fax software, 192
automating access, **226–227**

B

background operations
  fax, 15, 192, 200, 248
  modem, 46
backplates, 50, *51*

basic services on CompuServe, 33
.BAT files, 164
baud, 4, 249
BBS. *See* bulletin board systems (BBS)
Bell 103 standard, 8
Best of America Online button, 123, *124*
binary files, 165
bits, 249
bits per second (bps), **4–5**, 249
blocks in file transfers, 165–166, 249
.BMP files, 220
buffers, 249
bulletin board systems (BBS), 153–154, 249
  costs of, **162**
  finding, **155–157**
  getting online, **157–158**
  for Internet Access, 139
  navigating, **159–162**
  pluses and minuses of, **154–155**
  problems with, 214
  transferring files on, **171**
bundled software, **33**
button bar for WinCIM, **105–110**
buying modems, **27–28**
  at chain stores, **30**
  at computer stores, **30–31**
  by mail, **28–30**
bytes, 249

C

%C modem command, 234
cables, 20
  connecting, **41**

enrolling
   on America Online, **121**
   on CompuServe, **100–102**,
      101–102
   on Prodigy, **85–86**, *85*
error-correction. *See* protocols
escape sequence (+++), 231
exchange policies, 30
exclamation points (!) as modem
   command, 232
.EXE files, 220
extended services on Compu-
   Serve, 33
extended warranties, 32
extension phones, 23–24, 215
external modems, **11–13**, *11*, 251
   installing, **37–41**
   troubleshooting, **209**
Extra Fees features on Prodigy, 91

F

&F modem command, 211, 233
factory profiles, modem command for, 233
fall-back, 251
FAQ (Frequently Asked Questions)
   for Gopher, 144, *145*
   for help, 149
Favorite Places on CompuServe,
   104, *105*, 106
fax alerts, 192
fax machines
   vs. fax modems, **15**, **189–191**
   phone lines for, 25
fax modems, **14**, **187–188**
   answering problems with, 215
   Eclipse for, **197–200**, *198–199*

vs. fax machines, **15**, **189–191**
Faxability Plus for, **200**, *201*
software for, 14, **58**, **191–203**
speed of, 5
standards for, 14, **188–189**
WinFax for, **194–197**
WordPerfect 6 for DOS for,
   202, *203*
Fax/Paper Mail service on
   America Online, 130
Fax Services window (Word-
   Perfect), **202**, *202*
Faxability Plus program, 18, 58,
   200, *201*
Faxability Plus/OCR program, 58,
   200
File Transfer Protocol (FTP),
   146–147
file transfers. *See* transferring files
file viewers, 72
filing cabinet on CompuServe,
   108, *108*
finding
   bulletin boards, **155–157**
   CompuServe topics, 106
   Internet files, 148
   Internet users, **148**
   PKZIP and PKUNZIP
      programs, **221**
Finger utility, **148**
flow control, 213
forums, 252
Free features on Prodigy, 91
freeware, 225, 252
Frequently Asked Questions
   (FAQ)
   for Gopher, 144, *145*
   for help, 149

FTP (File Transfer Protocol),
146–147
full-duplex, 7, 251

G

garbage on screen, 212–214
gateways, 138, 252
GENERAL folder on Compu-
Serve, 108
.GIF File Viewers, 72, **222–225**, *224*
.GIF files, 164
glossary, **247–258**
Go To menu for America Online, 123
Gopher program, **143–144**,
144–145, **147**
Gopherspace, 148
gov domain on Internet, 150
graphics conversions in fax software, 192
graphics files
compressing, 220
viewers for, 72, **222–225**, *224*
Group 1 transmission standard,
188, 252
Group 2 transmission standard,
188, 252
Group 3 transmission standard,
14, 188–189, 252
Group 4 transmission standard,
189, 252
guarantees, 29, **32**

H

H modem command, 232
half-duplex, 7, 252
hand-shaking, 252
handles on America Online,
121, 123

hanging up, modem command
for, 232
hard drive space
planning for, **18–19**
for software, 71
hardware interrupts, **22–23**, **45–48**
Hayes command set, **229–236**
Hayes compatibility, 6, 253
help
on America Online, 129, 132
on CompuServe, 110
on Internet, **149**
on Prodigy, 94
highlight settings on Prodigy, 87
Home Office program, **204**
host computers, 181, *181–182*, 253
hypertext services, 149

I

IDs, problems with, 212
In basket on CompuServe, 107
inactivity timer, modem command for, 234
index on Prodigy, 88–89, *88*
indicator lights, 12
Industry Connection button on
America Online, 125, *126*
information superhighway, 135
initialization strings, 209
initializing, 253
Insert Variable dialog box (Win-
Fax), 197, *197*
installing
America Online software,
116–120
CompuServe software,
99–100, *100–101*
external modems, **37–41**

registers, modem, **234–236**
remote computing, **179–185,**
    181–184, 214
repeated characters, 213
repeating modem commands, 230
research on Internet, 138
resource guide, **241–245**
restocking fees, 29
restricting access
    on America Online, **133**
    on Prodigy, 93
result codes, modem command
    for, 233
return policies, 28, 30
RJ-11 plugs and connectors, 23,
    255
Rockwell chip set, 5
Royston, Pete, 94–95, 226
RTS/CTS flow control, 213

S

S registers, **234–236**
SatisFAXtion modems, 23, 58
scan and fax options in fax soft-
    ware, 192
scanners, 15, 189–191
scheduled transmissions in fax
    software, 192
sci news group, 137
screen names on America Online,
    121, 123
screwdrivers, 50
script languages, 71, 255
searching
    for bulletin boards, **155–157**
    for CompuServe topics, 106
    for Internet files, 148
    for Internet users, **148**

for PKZIP and PKUNZIP pro-
    grams, **221**
selecting
    phone numbers, **225–226**
    ports, **45–48**
    software, **71–72**
self-extracting files, 132, 220
semicolons (;) as modem com-
    mand, 231
Send Fax dialog box (Eclipse),
    198, *198*
Send Fax dialog box (Faxability),
    200, *201*
Send File Message dialog box
    (WinCIM), 168, *168*
serial connectors, 21, 22, 41
serial ports, 12, 250
    cable for, 41
    planning for, **19–23**
    problems with, 210
    in remote computing, 183
    selecting, **45–48**
Services window (CompuServe),
    105, *106*
Session Settings dialog box
    (CompuServe), 101–102,
    102, 104
setting up internal modems,
    45–48
settings, 255
Setup America Online dialog box
    (America Online), 117, *118*
shareware, 255
    for GIF viewers, 225
    Microlink, **69–70**, *69*
    PKZIP, 127, **132**, **220–222**
shells for Internet, **149**
shipping costs, 28
shopping cards on Prodigy, 87

GET A FREE CATALOG JUST FOR EXPRESSING YOUR OPINION.

Help us improve our books and get a *FREE* full-color catalog in the bargain. Please complete this form, pull out this page and send it in today. The address is on the reverse side.

Name _____ **Company** _____

Address _____ **City** _____ **State** ____ **Zip** _____

Phone (___) _____

1. How would you rate the overall quality of this book?

- ❏ Excellent
- ❏ Very Good
- ❏ Good
- ❏ Fair
- ❏ Below Average
- ❏ Poor

2. What were the things you liked most about the book? (Check all that apply)

- ❏ Pace
- ❏ Format
- ❏ Writing Style
- ❏ Examples
- ❏ Table of Contents
- ❏ Index
- ❏ Price
- ❏ Illustrations
- ❏ Type Style
- ❏ Cover
- ❏ Depth of Coverage
- ❏ Fast Track Notes

3. What were the things you liked *least* about the book? (Check all that apply)

- ❏ Pace
- ❏ Format
- ❏ Writing Style
- ❏ Examples
- ❏ Table of Contents
- ❏ Index
- ❏ Price
- ❏ Illustrations
- ❏ Type Style
- ❏ Cover
- ❏ Depth of Coverage
- ❏ Fast Track Notes

4. Where did you buy this book?

- ❏ Bookstore chain
- ❏ Small independent bookstore
- ❏ Computer store
- ❏ Wholesale club
- ❏ College bookstore
- ❏ Technical bookstore
- ❏ Other _____

5. How did you decide to buy this particular book?

- ❏ Recommended by friend
- ❏ Recommended by store personnel
- ❏ Author's reputation
- ❏ Sybex's reputation
- ❏ Read book review in _____
- ❏ Other _____

6. How did you pay for this book?

- ❏ Used own funds
- ❏ Reimbursed by company
- ❏ Received book as a gift

7. What is your level of experience with the subject covered in this book?

- ❏ Beginner
- ❏ Intermediate
- ❏ Advanced

8. How long have you been using a computer?

years _____

months _____

9. Where do you most often use your computer?

- ❏ Home
- ❏ Work

- ❏ Both
- ❏ Other _____

10. What kind of computer equipment do you have? (Check all that apply)

- ❏ PC Compatible Desktop Computer
- ❏ PC Compatible Laptop Computer
- ❏ Apple/Mac Computer
- ❏ Apple/Mac Laptop Computer
- ❏ CD ROM
- ❏ Fax Modem
- ❏ Data Modem
- ❏ Scanner
- ❏ Sound Card
- ❏ Other _____

11. What other kinds of software packages do you ordinarily use?

- ❏ Accounting
- ❏ Databases
- ❏ Networks
- ❏ Apple/Mac
- ❏ Desktop Publishing
- ❏ Spreadsheets
- ❏ CAD
- ❏ Games
- ❏ Word Processing
- ❏ Communications
- ❏ Money Management
- ❏ Other _____

12. What operating systems do you ordinarily use?

- ❏ DOS
- ❏ OS/2
- ❏ Windows
- ❏ Apple/Mac
- ❏ Windows NT
- ❏ Other _____

13. On what computer-related subject(s) would you like to see more books?

_____

_____

_____

14. Do you have any other comments about this book? (Please feel free to use a separate piece of paper if you need more room)

_____

_____

_____

_____

PLEASE FOLD, SEAL, AND MAIL TO SYBEX

SYBEX INC.
Department M
2021 Challenger Drive
Alameda, CA
94501

OIC, It's On-Line Shorthand!

On-line services are full of shorthand including "smileys" (shown on the inside front cover of this book), and TLAs (three-letter acronyms) that have now been augmented by MLAs (multiple-letter acronyms). Each bulletin board and forum has its own favorites, so you won't see all of the ones below used everywhere. But you'll see acronyms used wherever you go online.

AOL	America Online
ASAP	As soon as possible
BBS	Bulletin board system
BCNU	Be seeing you
BBL	Be back later
BRB	Be right back
BTW	By the way
CIS	CompuServe Information Service
DL	Download
FAQ	Frequently asked questions
FWIW	For what it's worth
FYI	For your information
GDR	Grinning, ducking, and running
IAC	In any case
IAE	In any event
IANAL	I am not a lawyer (usually followed by "but…" as in "IANAL, but it seems to me….")
IMCO	In my considered opinion
IMHO	In my humble opinion
IOW	In other words
LOL	Laughing out loud
LOLSCOK	Laughing out loud, spitting coffee on the keyboard
LOLSTC	Laughing out loud, scaring the cat